Motorcycle touring

Motorcycle touring

Peter 'the Bear' Thoeming and
Peter Rae

Published in 1982 by Osprey Publishing Limited,
12–14 Long Acre, London WC2E 9LP
Member company of the George Philip Group

British Library Cataloguing in Publication Data
Thoeming, Peter
    Motorcycle touring.
    1. Motorcycling – Great Britain
    I. Title   II. Rae, Peter
    796.7   GV1059.5
ISBN 0-85045-436-0

Editor Tim Parker
Design Norman Broadsword

Filmset and printed by Butler and Tanner Limited,
Frome, Somerset

Contents

	Introduction	7
Chapter 1	Touring in your own back yard: Ireland and Britain	10
Chapter 2	Riding farther afield: Continental Europe	26
Chapter 3	'Why don't we go to see the Guinness brewery?': Sydney to Singapore	48
Chapter 4	Conquering the Paper Tiger: South-East Asia	58
Chapter 5	So this is Shangri-La?: Nepal and India	68
Chapter 6	Where Islam rules: Pakistan to Turkey	78
Chapter 7	'Play Ramona again, Sam': Greece to Ireland	92
Chapter 8	Chasing the sun for winter: Britain to Spain	98
Chapter 9	Here's the Sahara but where's the scenery?: Morocco to Tunisia	110
Chapter 10	There are roads—and roads: Sicily to Greece	126
Chapter 11	'Your bike has just turned turtle...': Athens to London via the Eastern Bloc	138
Chapter 12	Full dress for the road: the American approach	150
Chapter 13	'You came all this way on *that*?' New York to San Francisco	158
	Epilogue	186
	Appendix	187
	Index	189

For Annie, Chris and Charlie, who put up with us

Introduction

'Roam abroad in the world, and take thy fill
of its enjoyments before the day shall come
when thou must quit it for good'—Sa'Di, 1258

TRAVEL HAS BEEN one of man's prime motivators since long before Columbus set sail for America. It is only in the latter half of this century, however, that the means of travelling has been readily available to anyone with a less pressing taste for adventure than Magellan or Marco Polo. The great travellers of history became legends in their own lifetimes as they opened up new frontiers—cultural and scientific as well as geographic. Today their names are respected in classrooms throughout the world they helped develop: Raleigh, Cook, Scott, Johnson, Alcock, Brown, Aerhart. Any schoolboy will attest to their courage, endurance, ingenuity and perseverance in the face of appalling adversity.

Today you or I can travel the same routes in a day or less, suffering no more than a mild case of jetlag or perhaps a missing suitcase. A Boeing 747 can have you in Paris for breakfast, New York for lunch and Los Angeles for supper, and the only discomfort you risk is indigestion from all that airline food. Modern travel focuses on the destination rather than the journey, and therein lies its popular appeal. It's fun, it's easy and it's not very expensive, but you sure miss out on an awful lot of people and places in between.

If you want to meet those people and see those places then the cabin of a Laker DC10 suddenly becomes a hopelessly inadequate vehicle from which to conquer the globe. The only answer is to get out there on the highways of the world and see the landscape changing before your eyes, feel its texture, sense its smells and learn from its people, in the shops, restaurants and petrol stations.

You can achieve some of that in a coach, but coaches always seem to encapsulate the atmosphere of their country of embarkation: board a coach in London with a group of other Londoners and, no matter how far that coach travels, you still end up with a rolling bubble of British culture which places you at a distance from the countryside that you are passing through. The tour guide or courier is an effective barrier between you and your new environment: you board to his schedule, eat to his schedule and stop where he decides. If the coach is air-conditioned you can't even open a window to savour the sweet scent of the orange groves flashing past on your left. No, a coach is little improvement on an aircraft cabin.

A car is a different proposition: you can open all the windows you want, stop where you wish, eat where you like and generally be a free agent. Yes, there's a lot to be said for touring by car—until you've been touring by motorcycle. Motorcycles give their riders an unmatched sense of well-being, freedom and independence. Sure, they're also economical, easy to park, cheaper to take on ferries and can go places no car could ever hope to reach; but, by and large, that's not why people are buying them in such rapidly increasing numbers the world over. People buy motorcycles because they are fun to ride: period. All other reasons are secondary at best, or excuses at worst.

Touring by motorcycle shows you the world as you have never seen it before. You become part of the earth's tantalizing tapestry and its threads are all the more vivid because of the effect your passing has on the many weavers. People everywhere treat the long-distance motorcyclist with a respectful curiosity rarely shown to ordinary tourists. This respect is born of the knowledge that he is open and vulnerable to a strange environment in a way that few modern travellers are. On a motorcycle you are open to strangers in so many ways: you are at the mercy of their unusual driving habits; your personal belongings are open to their gaze; your eyes are open to their blemishes, your ears to their languages, your nose to their smells. Your face feels their breezes and your back the heat of their sun. And if things go wrong you can't scurry into the cultural cocoon of your air-conditioned coach or wind up the windows of your car to isolate yourself and make contact impossible. In fact, in southern European and Third World countries where Western man is often regarded as 'soft', there is a widespread appreciation that the long-distance motorcyclist has achieved something difficult in just getting there. This unplanned exhibition of sheer competence automatically places the rider several steps ahead of his plane-, car-, and coach-bound counterparts. All in all, there are fewer barriers between the motorcyclist and the locals and friendships are easier to strike up as a result.

Motorcycle touring has a tangible romanticism that stems directly from close contact with new people and places. You know you are seeing them for the first and probably the last time, but their memory stays with you long after you've scraped the dead flies from your headlight and settled down again—temporarily—to the daily routine. The experienced motorcycle traveller ends up with a series of images and memories that really transcend borders, oceans and time zones. He is aware that while the waitress in a small truck stop in El Centro, California, is pouring the first black coffee of the day, her counterpart in Rhinebeck, New York, is preparing for the lunchtime rush; at the same time the main roads out of London are clogged with the evening traffic; crisp, white tablecloths are being laid over wooden tables in Sorrento's bayside restaurants; the Sikh watchmen are making their midnight security rounds in Calcutta's dockland and young couples are already watching the spectacular sunrise on a new day from Cape Byron, Australia's eastern most point.

Being able to relate the small happenings of life to the whole is one of the benefits of this micro-view of the world as seen from the saddle of a motorcycle. If travel broadens the mind—as it must—then travel by motorcycle enriches the learning process by bringing the mind that much closer to new people, new cultures and new ideas.

It was motorcycles that brought the Bear and I together in the first place. He had just arrived in London after a seven-month motorcycle trip from Sydney. I was editing a motorcycle magazine at the time and he offered to write the story of his marathon adventure for me. It became clear immediately that we both shared the same love of motorcycles and motorcycle touring. Furthermore, we found we are both motivated by a common wanderlust and a strong belief that nothing could better epitomize a wasted life than to die without ever seeing the splendour of the Alps, the majesty of Mt Kilimanjaro at sunrise, the bustling street life of India, the solitude of the Australian outback or the spellbinding beauty of the Monterey peninsula at sunset.

Veteran motorcycle tourer and magazine editor John McDermott puts it like this: 'What I like best about touring is that while you're doing it you're travelling and not arriving somewhere. You are experiencing some strange part of the world and you are not involved with anything else. And you really get back to basics. The problems you meet on tour are real problems; the sort of problems you have at home pale into insignificance.'

It is at that stage that you realize that the journey has become at least as important as the destination. You are a participant among the ever-changing scenery of life's stage, rather than a mere spectator. We hope you are now ready to participate in our two-wheeled odyssey across five continents, to enjoy one of the last real adventures open to modern man—and perhaps be tempted to follow in our tyre tracks.

Chapter 1

Touring in your own back yard

Ireland and Britain

THE NARROW ROAD twisted, turned, snaked and climbed tortuously through the Wicklow mountains. Snow-covered fields on either side rolled endlessly away into the hills, blinding white in the early March afternoon. A pale yellow sun hung low in a cloudless eggshell-blue sky, bathing the entire fairytale scene in a picturesque glow, but doing nothing to raise the temperature more than a degree or two above freezing.

Four small motorcycles pressed on towards the summit, swinging sinuously from side to side in tune with the sweeping bends, the only moving objects on the desolate landscape. We hadn't passed a car in miles or seen a living soul since Aughavanagh slipped past in our mirrors. The snow ploughs had been out and the roads were damp from the melting snow, but clear. Kevin was in the lead on his Honda 175, keeping warm with his regulation two pairs of trousers and socks, three sweaters, two pairs of gloves, thick scarf, heavy boots and Barbour jacket. Séamus was shivering to death on the pillion, his skinny frame covered only in thin cotton trousers, one sweater, a short anorak and walking shoes. He really looked as if he might suffer from exposure if we didn't find shelter soon. Denis wasn't much better off; just as his 175 relied on string and wire to stay together, so he too depended on two elastic bands around the cuffs of his casual leather jacket to keep the wind at bay. Such ingenious refinements were not to be found around the wide open cuffs of my double-breasted car coat, and the chill breeze played cruel games around my wrists, up the sleeves and down the billowing back. As I leaned my newly acquired and rare 1963 CB92 Sports Benly through the corners just ahead of Brendan's Honda 90, my chattering teeth created a greater racket than the high-revving engine below.

It was a fine day. In Ireland, when the sun shines it's always a fine day—whatever the temperature. The appearance of that glowing orb in Irish skies is such an unusual occurrence that all lovers of the outdoors have to make the most of every opportunity. That's precisely what we were doing, but even I questioned our collective sanity as we crested the rise near the Turlough Hill hydroelectric power station and dropped down into the next valley, heading back towards Dublin, home and warmth before the sun finally dropped below the horizon, taking with it the last illusions of friendliness and comfort.

The fun part of the ride was well and truly over and from there on the trip became an ordeal to be finished with as quickly as possible. We went

Homeward bound! This Belgian couple are all smiles as they head for the Dover car ferry on the ubiquitous and excellent Honda Gold Wing De Luxe

our separate ways at Stillorgan, elated but dangerously cold. Back in the warmth of the Rae family kitchen it was a good half-hour before sufficient feeling returned to my frigid digits to let me pour a cup of badly needed hot coffee. Instead, I killed the time in front of the gas fire looking at the map to see where we'd been. It was the first time I had ventured any distance on my motorcycle and I was keen to find out just how many miles we'd clocked up.

We'd ridden 75 miles! We laugh now, looking back, but I was so ecstatic I called Denis to break the good news! When you're 17 with your first real bike and your usual riding beat rarely extends beyond suburbia, then covering 75 miles in an afternoon just for fun is something of which you can be justly proud.

That was really my first experience of motorcycle 'touring', but as the weather grew warmer so the distances grew longer. Almost every Sunday we would ride somewhere—anywhere—just for the joy of riding. Wicklow, Arklow, Wexford; 80 miles, 100 miles, 150 miles. One Saturday morning we even rode the 202 miles to Belfast and back simply to buy a Barbour jacket. A lot of folks said we were crazy: maybe they were right. A lot of folks still say we're crazy: maybe they're still right.

The important thing was that I was getting out there on my bike and seeing new countryside. We used to call it 'going for a gruel' for some inexplicable reason—possibly because, on our old bikes, it was pretty gruelling—but it was touring at its most basic. Sure, we'd sit back and watch numbers of the Dublin Motorcycle Tour Club blast past on their new Honda 750s, BMWs and a lone Moto Guzzi V7 Ambassador *en route* to some far-flung corner of the land at intergalactic speed. We'd sit there on our slightly ratty little Hondas and hold forth at great length on why we'd never bother with such-and-such a superbike for touring, but we each knew precisely which bike we'd buy for that Big Trip.

Being realists as well as dreamers, however, we stayed for the time being with our little bikes and little trips. It was the first of many lessons learned over the years to be proved true time and time again: you don't need a large engine or a specialized touring bike to go touring. It makes the journey easier in many ways, but it sure ain't essential.

What is essential is a certain degree of wanderlust, that strong desire to experience as much of the world beyond your own back door as possible. That's the basic ingredient: the only other indispensable item is some kind of powered two-wheeled transport. From there on, everything else can be added as funds permit or preference dictates. The large motorcycle, quickly detachable matching luggage, fairing, stereo cassette player and all the other touring luxuries can be added to the touring rider's equipment in the fullness of time. Before that he'll need to have sorted out something in the way of weatherproof clothing—especially if his touring will take him anywhere near north-western Europe in general and the British Isles in particular!

It was with only the basic necessities—125cc Honda sports bike, the hypothermia-inducing car coat and a king-size appetite for travel—that I set out to explore my own back yard, which just happened to be the

13

British Isles. Despite their reputation for cold and wet weather, Ireland and Britain have a great deal to offer the touring motorcyclist. The Irish Republic, in fact, is one of the finest motorcycling countries. Being born there and having lived there for 20 years may have coloured my judgement slightly, but the place has the same effect on every overseas touring rider I've met who has ventured across the Irish Sea. For a start, the whole pace of life in Ireland remains slower than in any other Western nation; the Italians may get less done, but they make a lot more noise and fuss doing it!

Ireland, on the other hand, makes a virtue out of relaxation. Where else but in Kerry would the petrol station attendant pop out from his house to ask if you wouldn't mind waiting half an hour for a fill-up— while he watched the All-Ireland Hurling Final on TV! And where else, I ask you, would you come across the approach to a sharp bend with the word SLOW written on the road in big white letters and 50 yards farther on find the word SLOWER! Little off-beat things like that crop up everywhere to enrich the touring experience. But what makes Ireland a motorcyclist's paradise is the roads. Motorways are non-existent and dual carriageways rare. In their place are many thousands of miles of well-surfaced two-lane and single-track roads that wind, rise, fall and sweep through some of the most spectacular and unspoilt scenery in Europe. And you can really *ride* those twisting tracts of tarmac because Ireland is one of the Western World's most sparsely populated countries. A mere three and a half million souls are scattered across an area almost the size of England and a third of those live in and around the capital, Dublin.

Ireland is an increasingly prosperous nation these days, but its citizens haven't quite reached the dizzy California heights of 2·4 cars per person. The result is that the motorcyclist has the road virtually to himself in rural areas and towns and villages are few and far between compared with England. In fact, after you've ridden for half an hour in the more remote parts without seeing a car or truck you can come to resent any intrusion on *your* road. Cruising speed is largely a matter of how you feel at the time, because the chances of being stopped for speeding are very slim indeed. The overall limit is 60mph, but you can count the number of radar traps in operation on the fingers of one hand and you'll hardly ever see a police car on the open road. Besides, the police have had a lot more serious things on their minds since the escalation of terrorist violence in Northern Ireland.

The comparatively light traffic flow can have its drawbacks, though. Irish car drivers have little experience of the dense traffic conditions in the rest of Europe and their road sense lacks that sharp edge that the rest of us have come to depend on for survival. Even in the cities, lane discipline is appalling; it's almost as if the highway code had specified that everybody should drive in the outside lane. Highway code? What am I talking about? In 1979 the government got so far behind with its driving test programme that it overcame the backlog by granting a full licence to thousands of learners without any test!

The mists of Dover are one of many good reasons for crossing back over Channel to France. Most Europeans settle for tank bag and panniers rather than the 'full-dress' alternative

It's not uncommon to see cars driving around on bald tyres with body panels hanging on by the strength of their rust spots. And you need to beware of distinctly Irish driving idiosyncrasies. My good friend and colleague Bruce Preston, chairman of the 50,000-strong British Motorcyclists Federation, once came steaming around a bend on his BMW to find the road ahead completely blocked by two tractors, the drivers of which had stopped side by side for a chat! If he gave them a piece of his mind as he slewed to a halt, they didn't seem too upset.

You might not always be that lucky, however. On a rare short-cut through strife-torn Northern Ireland, *en route* from picturesque Donegal's north-west tip to Dublin, my wife Chris and I had the fright of our lives on our CBX. After a remarkably trouble-free trip, we arrived in the border town of Newry to find armed troops and police everywhere. As we rode slowly and deliberately down one street, a soldier followed our every move through the sights of a swivel-mounted machine gun on the back of a flat-bed Land-Rover. I think we both felt more than a mite nervous as we thought of the consequences of a single backfire from the motorcycle. But as we followed a heavily patrolled diversion route it turned out that the cause of all the activity was a fatal road accident. The security forces, however, were taking no chances. Then, as a flak-jacketed

Deserted roads and old village pumps are two of the attractions for touring riders in Ireland

police officer, gun at his side, waved us forward, the lady driver in front stalled her car on the hill and started to roll back down the hill towards my front wheel. I gave a couple of toots on the horn to warn her of the impending contact and was met with the most vicious hail of verbal abuse I'd heard in my life! She managed to restart, but continued to curse me roundly out of her open window, totally unconcerned by the presence of a very young girl sitting next to her. As I pulled out to overtake, she did her damnedest to run me right off the road, red-faced and beside herself with anger. If anyone ever tries to tell you that nobody *needs* 105bhp and sub-12-second quarter-mile acceleration on a motorcycle, tell them about this pleasant little interlude in Ulster. We rode the last few miles to the Irish border in a controlled panic, and didn't breathe freely again until we were safely back in the South.

Not long afterwards we saw that a woman passenger in a car had been shot dead by a nervous guard at an army checkpoint near the border at Strabane, which we had passed through earlier in the day on that same trip. Now wild horses couldn't drag me back into Northern Ireland until the terrorist street war there is at an end. It's a great shame, for the North has its share of spectacular scenery—the Giant's Causeway in Antrim is one unique example—and the roads and signposting are better than in the South. But touring by bike has enough normal hazards without unnecessarily adding the prospect of being shot or blown up.

Back in southern Ireland there's more than enough to keep the touring rider fully occupied. Dublin itself has many attractions besides the Guinness brewery that drew The Bear like a magnet all the way from Sydney (see Chapter 4). Trinity College is a green oasis of learning in the city centre and nearby Merrion Square boasts examples of some of the finest remaining Georgian houses in the world. You can sup creamy stout in such cultural centres as O'Donoghue's in Merrion Row or the Old Bailey off fashionable Grafton Street; visit Sandymount Strand and relive *Ulysses;* or ride the few short miles out to the James Joyce museum in a Martello Tower at Dun Laoghaire. South of Dublin are numerous beauty spots like the Vico Road at Dalkey and Killiney Hill with its panoramic views and luxury houses. By now you're almost in County Wicklow, with some of the best motorcycling country in Europe. The road through the Glen of the Downs is an almost flat-out delight and leads to the coastal route to Brittas Bay with its numerous secluded beaches and coves.

No touring rider's visit to this part of the world is complete without a trip out into the Dublin/Wicklow mountains. The road through Sally Gap, Roundwood, Laragh, Glenmalure and Aughavanagh is a living tapestry of winding asphalt, gorse-covered hills and beautiful lakes that is breathtaking in summer and awesome at any other time. Much the same scenery can be found in other parts of the country, except that in Kerry, Clare and Killarney it is tempered with a rounded softness, while in Donegal it has a menacing stark brutality that deserves to be experienced. Last time we visited this outpost of Western Europe we braved Force 7 winds riding out to the tip of Bloody Foreland, a desolate peninsula at Ireland's north-western extremity. On a wet winter's day you could be forgiven for thinking that you were all alone in the universe up here; better to visit in summer and make the most of the many miles of unspoilt and deserted beaches. The roads have their own inbuilt speed limit in Donegal; they are built over bogland that has allowed the surface to sink every few feet to produce an endless series of washboard ripples that is more than a match for any standard motorcycle suspension system much over 40mph!

Donegal is also one of the few parts of the country where you can walk into a shop and find everyone but yourself talking in an incomprehensible tongue—Irish. English is the primary language of Ireland—educated Dubliners still claim that the best English is spoken in the capital—and although Irish is still taught to all schoolchildren it lives on only in subsidized *Gaeltacht* areas. Elsewhere it is largely forgotten.

Apart from Donegal, Connemara is the main Irish-speaking area and a must for the visiting motorcyclist. It comprises the bulk of the mid-western seaboard near Galway and it's a mere morning's ride from Dublin, so you can travel coast-to-coast before lunch. The narrow roads pass through sparsely populated farming regions. Cold lakes lap lazily on one side of the road while green and purple mountains rise in the middle distance. Mountains abound: there's Croagh Patrick, where thousands of religious pilgrims—some on their knees, others with bare feet bleeding on the rough shale—make the annual climb to hear Mass in the church on the summit; the majestic Twelve Bens; and then you're into Joyce Country and a wealth of literary history near Ben Bulban. All around are stone-walled fields with numerous piles of cut and drying turf. Plumes of smoke from turf fires in thatched cottages fill the air with the sweet smell of burning peat to be remembered long afterwards. The coast is peppered with vast expanses of clean, white sand that is invariably deserted—even at the height of the season. Swimming is not among the achievements of the locals, many of whom make their living by fishing from hand-made boats known as currachs—a more unstable, capsizeable boat is hard to imagine.

In fine weather it's paradise, but even in the rain it retains an inescapable charm. Its attractions had drawn me back time and time again on smaller machines before I rode over to Roundstone one particularly wet December day on a BMW R100S to visit an old family friend, the late Prince Milo of Montenegro. The Prince had settled in this little Connemara fishing village in the 1940s after years in exile from his native Montenegro following its takeover by the Communists in the early part of the century; Montenegro is one of the six former states that make up present-day Yugoslavia. Prince Milo, whose sister was the last Queen of Italy, had lived for a time in the United States and China, among other places, before moving to the tranquillity of the West of Ireland, where he collected *objets d'art*. Finding him in good spirits, we talked about his fascinating life and the beauty of his adopted homeland. As I was leaving he reached up and lifted down one of the many oil paintings from the walls of his old cottage and insisted that I accept it as a gift. I was

Inveterate tourers Bruce and Brenda Preston are well used to ending up on deserted beaches in the west of Ireland; but it helps to know which deserted beach you're on . . .

staggered by his generosity—it was a lovely work—but pointed out that I had to ride 200 miles home in the continuing torrential downpour on a motorcycle. The painting looked just too large to fit inside one of my Krauser panniers. But the Prince had an answer to that one: he explained that it was a seventeenth-century work in oil on copper by Jan Horremans, a Flemish painter, and would come to no harm, as he would wrap it in cardboard, brown paper and twine!

And so it was a wet and bedraggled figure on a red BMW steered a shaky passage over streaming Connemara lanes with surely the strangest cargo ever to travel by motorcycle. After 50 miles I stopped at the first outpost of civilization, the town of Oughterard, and invested in a large black plastic dustbin liner to protect the 300-year-old painting on its last 150 miles in the worst rain the Emerald Isle could offer. It still hangs on the wall of my living-room as a constant reminder of that unusual journey!

Although they may not all give away old masters to passing motorcyclists, the Irish are friendly and warm to strangers and seem less inclined to turn up their noses at motorcyclists than, say, the English. One sure way to get into conversation with the locals is to go into a pub— any pub. The licensing hours are particularly liberal: official closing time is 11.30pm in summer with 10 minutes' drinking-up time. But outside the big towns, actual closing time depends on the attitude and alcoholic

The only problem with tank bags is that you have to shift them to fill the tank. This one is easier to cope with than some

preferences of the local police and drinking can continue into the wee small hours.

Any touring rider in Britain or visiting the British Isles should seriously consider taking a bike to Ireland. Four ferries ply the sometimes rough stretch of water separating Ireland from Britain. Sealink runs one from Fishguard to Rosslare and another from Holyhead to Dun Laoghaire, while the B&I line runs boats from Liverpool to Dublin and Swansea to Cork. Both companies run a good service, although the boats are not on a par with some of the better cross-Channel ferries. The Sealink routes tend to be slightly less costly and the journey times shorter, while the B&I ports in the UK are slightly easier to reach by road. Continental riders may save both time and money by investigating the ferry service that runs direct from Le Havre to Rosslare. However, riders from the United States or farther afield shouldn't plan to fly in and buy a bike in Ireland with a view to taking it on to Britain and the Continent. Motorcycles in Ireland cost roughly a third more than the same motorcycle in England, and the available insurance cover is less comprehensive and far more costly. Far better to buy the bike in London and *then* tackle Ireland.

Of course, if you're starting off in Britain—either as a visitor or a resident just finding your touring legs—then there's a great variety of things to see and do in England, Scotland and Wales. Foreign visitors are so well catered for that it's often the neophyte resident tourer who needs a little encouragement. The logic of touring with whatever you've got (the Americans have a colourful phrase for it in racing circles: 'run what ya brung') still applies. As long as it's over 50cc and you hold a full driving licence then Britain's motorway network is open to take you wherever you want to go—if getting there is the main concern.

I think the main benefit of motorways to touring riders in Britain is that they take all the commercial and much of the holiday traffic off the excellent A and B class roads, leaving the motorcyclist relatively free to enjoy the much more interesting perspective which these roads can offer. But I suppose London and the Home Counties tend to be one of the biggest draws for overseas riders, being within easy reach of the Channel ports. When I visit Rome by bike I am interested in seeing the same sights as the rest of the tourists: St Peter's, the Forum, the Colosseum, the Vatican Museum, the Via Venito. By the same token, visiting motorcyclists from overseas want to see the Tower of London, Buckingham Palace, the Changing of the Guard, Tower Bridge, the Houses of Parliament, Hyde Park, Piccadilly Circus; then after lunch there's Madame Tussaud's Waxworks, half a dozen museums and art galleries, seedy Soho, numerous discount motorcycle dealers, cut-price accessory shops and 1001 different ways to eat and drink the night away.

But, when all is said and done, London is a big city much like any other; culture vultures apart, there's a lot to see and do outside. The Home Counties (Kent, Surrey, Sussex, Essex, Hertfordshire and Middlesex) are fairly densely populated and mostly flat. Touring interest centres mainly around historic houses such as Churchill's former home at Chartwell, near Westerham in Kent, and the plethora of small English country pubs, inns and restaurants in this part of the world. But it's only when you move farther out from London that the scope really improves for the touring rider. Oxfordshire boasts the Great Ridgeway, one of Britain's oldest roads, which runs for 85 miles through some spectacular scenery, and although rutted and overgrown in parts is accessible to most touring bikes. It's a real hot potato in British motorcycling politics, however, and the scene of much behind-the-scenes conflict between motorcyclists and ramblers. Trail riders have agreed a voluntary code of practice that includes a 25mph speed limit, stopping to let horses pass, and no use on Sundays between May and October. It's worth a visit, for all that.

Nearby is the famous White Horse at Uffington Castle, while off to the west, in Hampshire, is the beautiful New Forest, which covers 92,000 acres. Wiltshire is renowned for such wonders as Stonehenge, a series of concentric stone circles dating from 1500BC. Then there's the Avebury Stone Circle dating from 1900BC and the prehistoric ceremonial centre of Woodhenge. Farther west lies the summer playground of Devon and Cornwall, with their beaches and subcultures of scuba divers, surfers and sailors.

A Honda CB400 makes a fine solo touring mount, especially on these 'B' roads which run the length and breadth of Britain

Perhaps the rural beauty of England is best typified by the Cotswolds to the north of Oxford, where the A34 winds its way over the hills and through quaint old English villages like Woodstock and Chipping Norton. In places like Bourton-on-the-Water, Moreton-in-Marsh, Lower and Upper Slaughter and Stow-on-the-Wold you can experience something of the grander style of English living, where afternoon tea served in fussy gardens includes scones with butter, strawberry jam and fresh whipped cream. Ah, that's the life! Besides good views of rolling green countryside in the Vale of Evesham and picturesque stone houses, the Cotswolds are very popular with well-heeled British holidaymakers. I remember once when we were touring the area on my XS750, Chris and I stayed at the very select Lygon Arms hotel in the little village of Broadway. While we were struggling into our waterproofs in the lobby one damp Sunday morning we caught a fascinating glimpse of how the other half lives. A gentleman in his late thirties asked a porter to load his suite of matching luggage into the boot of his gleaming Rolls-Royce, parked 20ft away just outside the main door. The porter dashed off to attend to some other urgent task before complying, while the Rolls owner leaned casually against the car for several minutes gazing at his luggage! Had he loaded his own bags he could have been on his way before the porter returned!

Wales is another area with much to offer the touring motorcyclist, especially North Wales and Snowdonia, where the marvellous A5 twists and climbs through a green and desolate landscape. Almost every time I ride in Wales the mists descend and cover the area in a blanket of bleak dampness—but for the most part that has been during the winter months. When the sun does shine, Wales is wonderful riding country. We hit the jackpot one October Saturday morning a couple of years back while returning from Ireland via Holyhead on a Honda CBX. It was a beautifully crisp morning and for some reason the roads through the mountains and down into the centre of Wales were deserted. Now dicing with death is never my favourite pastime, but at one stage we overtook a Ford Granada hearse (travelling 'empty' at the time!), which immediately tucked in behind and chased us across the countryside at speeds up to 90mph. We were all enjoying ourselves immensely, but I think the hearse driver was trying to rustle up a little business, because he started getting too close for comfort in the corners. I pulled over and slowed down to let him pass, but a mile or two up the road at Corwen he got stuck behind a caravan—and we left him for dead! We made the 300-odd mile trip from Holyhead to our home in Gravesend in a record 5 hours 10 minutes, proving that even the latest generation of 100bhp-plus superbikes are capable touring machines.

The Midlands region of England is heavily industrialized and offers little other than boredom for the touring rider, but Liverpool of course is the gateway to the Isle of Man, which becomes a motorcycling paradise for the first two weeks of June each year as host to the TT races. Some 15,000 riders flock to the Island on their bikes during this period, many of them from the Continent. The weather in the Irish Sea is always unpredictable, but TT regulars reckon it's worth risking a week of rain to soak up the unique atmosphere of life at the TT. The races form only a small part of the festivities: there are drag races, motocross, grass track events, trials and numerous motorcycle club rallies for owners of particular makes and models. For two weeks the Island lives, eats, sleeps and breathes motorcycles and motorcycling, and if you're into overdoses of both then it can be a hell of a good holiday. Most hotels and guest houses are booked up well in advance, so camping is probably a safer alternative for newcomers. Some riders prefer to avoid the seething mass of motorcyclists during race week and visit the Isle of Man earlier or later in the year, when they enjoy the roads, scenery and beaches to the full. As an added bonus, continental visitors planning to visit Scotland can sail direct from the Island to Ardrossan, cutting out the long and boring drag through the north of England by road. In fact, John Ross, a good friend who regards Scotland and the northern isles as his favourite touring preserve, reckons that the only problem with touring in Scotland is that most of us have to pass through the north of England to get there! It's not that bad, but it is uninspiring. Most people choose to get the trip over as quickly as possible by travelling up the M1/M6/A74, but that's boring in the extreme. A better route, and almost as quick, is to follow the A1 north to Scotch Corner and then take the A68 to Edinburgh.

Scotland is a hard day's ride from London and the south-east and riders with time on their hands may care to break their journey in the Lake District, a vast National Park in the north-west of England dotted with famous lakes such as Windermere and Derwent Water. This is fine motorcycling countryside with dozens of campsites and a good number of small hotels. The park includes several good roads open to motorcycles for those who like to get off the beaten track. The north of England in general and Scotland in particular are among the best parts of Britain for using high-performance machines with little risk of attracting too much attention from the police. A slight drawback in Scotland is the relative paucity of motorcycle dealers outside Glasgow, Edinburgh and Motherwell. Most shops cater mainly for enduro and trials bikes, but may be able to help standard touring riders with a bit of old-fashioned improvization.

For scenery try the west coast of Scotland first. It's a bit bleak in places but beautiful for all that, provided the weather is good. If it's not, the chances are that a ride eastwards will yield an improvement. When it's raining in one part of Scotland it can often be dry and sunny not too far away. The most interesting route up the west coast would be to follow the motorway to Stirling, turning off early to take the old road through Bannockburn. This is where the Scots achieved one of their few victories over the English back in 1314 and history fans can catch a blow-by-blow account at the tourist centre. Stirling, just up the road, is the gateway to the Highlands of Scotland and a good place to stay; its castle is one of the finest in Britain. Following the road on up to the Bridge of Allan takes you to the Wallace Monument, which must be reached on foot but is well worth the climb for the unparalleled view it

24

offers of the Highlands to the north. Then the ride to Fort William via Callander, Crianlarich, Tyndrum and Glencoe is one of the most enjoyable in Scotland, with camping available near the village of Glen Coe, although this is not an official site. The bridge at Balla is the quickest way to Fort William, but the longer route around Loch Leven is far more interesting.

The A830 from Fort William to Mallaig is possibly the finest motorcycling road in Scotland. The scenery is quite exceptional, even by Scottish standards, and the single-track ribbon of tarmac is known as the Road to the Isles as it leads to the islands of Skye and Harris. Skye is bleak and barren, but ideal for walkers and hill climbers. Ferries to the island take about 30 minutes and are run by Caledonian McBrane during the summer months only. The shorter hop from Kyle of Lochalsh to Kyleakin runs all year round, and a 'Hopscotch' multi-journey ticket is available for anyone planning to visit more than one island in the region. Accommodation is made easier to find throughout Scotland by an extensive room-finding service run by the tourist offices. A rider planning to stop overnight in all but the smallest towns can rely on this service, although in high season it's wise to contact the tourist office by 4pm in the larger towns. Two-star hotels in Scotland are normally much better than the equivalent rating in England or Wales and motorcyclists are made as welcome as anyone else. The following hotels are recommended: the Crianlarich Hotel in Crianlarich; the Invervey Hotel at Tyndrum, which makes up in friendly service what it lacks in luxury; and the Caledonian Hotel in Fort Augustus, the best of them all.

Touring in your own back yard has a number of advantages for the novice two-wheeled traveller: the trip can be tailored to fit a weekend or a week; it's generally the cheapest way to start touring; it's easier to get home if your bike or your backside proves unable to cope. But it's rarely long before you set your sights on more distant horizons and venture farther afield.

Chapter 2

Riding farther afield

Continental Europe

IF YOU'VE ENJOYED those first touring experiences close to home, you'll soon be straining at the leash to try more ambitious trips. If your home is in one of the larger American states then your immediate objective will be to cross the state line and explore a new environment; if your back yard happens to be New South Wales in Australia then you'll probably want to give Queensland a try; if, like me, your first faltering steps awheel were made in the British Isles you'll be itching to cross the English Channel and soak up some of the sunshine rumoured to exist on the other side!

Now you're entering real mainstream touring—the sort where you scrape together two or three weeks for your summer vacation, bribe your wife or girlfriend to ride pillion (or not, as the case may be!), and head off into the wild blue yonder. Not many of us get to The Bear's happy state of closing the door on job, family and friends for a couple of years and circumnavigating the globe, although his fascinating adventures may well trigger off just such a reaction in many readers. Most touring enthusiasts live all year round for those two summer weeks of unbridled bliss on foreign soil.

All touring riders must know the feeling: you finish work on the Friday evening, ride home, sort out the panniers and tank bag, convince your loved one that *this* year you're going to travel light; you pack the bags, ruthlessly decide that you won't need more than four shirts, hide your other half's heated rollers and fall into bed wondering what the hell you've forgotten. Up with the sun next morning, you toss razor and washbags into the tank bag, strap everything onto the bike while sipping a scalding hot cup of coffee; you check that you have the ferry tickets, passports, driving licence, Green Card insurance, petrol coupons, travellers' cheques, foreign currency, motorcycle registration document, maps and the key to the panniers. Then you reluctantly strap the waterproof gear to the carrier, knowing that it is unwanted weight, but also aware of the utter folly of leaving it behind. You switch off everything in the house, leave a note for the milkman and close the door on normal life for two weeks.

It's a fairly tense moment as you fire up and burble down the road, knowing that you're probably waking the neighbours but more worried that you've forgotten something vital. Some tension still lingers as you rush for the ferry (if continental Europe is your destination), trying to make up for those lost minutes as you dashed back indoors to find your sunglasses, but the tension is mitigated by the relaxed feeling of being on the road and on your way. I find I can start to really relax only after the mad dash to the ferry is over and the Channel is safely behind me. Then there's time to savour the new smells of the French countryside as you rumble peacefully down a tree-lined Route Nationale and feel light-years away from yesterday's humdrum problems.

The sense of personal freedom and exhilaration is the same at the beginning of any such trip, wherever you are. It's an adrenalin high that keeps you coming back for more, years after year. And the beauty of it is that you don't need the latest luxury touring machine with colour-co-ordinated luggage to sample that thrill for the first time. The same bike and equipment that took you on your travels nearer home will handle the longer trip nicely—you just need to be a little more thorough (all right, a lot more thorough) in your preparation, because a breakdown now could leave you stranded a long way from home, and repatriation of bike and rider could cost a fortune.

You can take this touring thing too seriously, though. I'll never forget a call I had a few years back from a BMF (British Motorcyclists Federation) member who wanted to know if anyone organized European tours with support trucks loaded with spare parts! He wanted to travel in a group for moral support, insure against every eventuality and be followed everywhere by a mobile parts shop. Ah, I thought, he probably has an old ex-War Department BSA M20 and is none too sure of its reliability ... but it turned out that he had an almost-new Honda 400/4! I tried to be as helpful as possible, but gently suggested that he risked eliminating all the fun from his trip by seeking to avoid all the hazards. I suppose you can err on the side of optimism, too. I tend to compromise a little these days, but my first foray across the Channel will remain one of the most memorable because it was so unplanned. I just got this urge to visit my sister in Rome, but cash was limited as I'd been out of college and working for less than a year. My bike at the time was a near-new Yamaha 350 YR5, designed more for scratching around twisty mountain roads and accelerating away from traffic lights than traversing continents, but it would have to do. Preparation consisted of an oil change and lubing and adjusting the chain. Luggage comprised a new tank bag from Lewis Leathers for £6 (this was 1975, when men were men and money had some value—ah, I remember it well), which was half-filled with clothing; the other half was taken up with a one-gallon can of two-stroke oil, because I knew it would cost three times as much in France and Italy.

The sole concession to organization was obtaining the necessary Italian translation of my British driving licence, a carefully calculated quantity of Italian petrol coupons (to cut petrol costs there by a third), Green Card insurance for £7.50 (this extends your full UK insurance cover to the countries you plan to visit) and general baggage insurance for £1.70. Oh, yes, and ferry tickets for the princely sum of £14. That was to be it. The only tools were the ones in the Yamaha's toolkit. I fully intended travelling in my denim jeans and leather jacket, but the collective pressure of my flatmates forced me to reconsider and strap a small tote bag containing a waterproof oversuit to the rear of the dualseat (and there it stayed until I returned to Dover two weeks later to be greeted by traditional summer rain!).

The euphoria of the pre-dawn rush to catch the car ferry at Dover lasted all day, boosted by the novelty of my new surroundings. The object was to get to Barbara's apartment in Rome—and free lodgings!— as quickly and cheaply as possible. So lunch was a Coke and some sandwiches prepared at my flat the night before, enjoyed in brilliant sunshine at the roadside. I was far from sure how far I'd get that first day, but at 5.30 that afternoon I trundled into Dijon after covering 450 miles since I started out. Such was my eagerness for the trip and the sheer pleasure of riding that when I saw a sign for Geneva I almost followed it, knowing that somewhere near my route through the Jura mountains was a youth hostel at Les Rousses. But good sense told me I was tired and in no fit state to start looking for a bed in strange mountains in twilight, so I settled instead for a small hotel and dinner in Dijon. The Yamaha's thin saddle was no ideal touring perch, but youthful exuberance helped me to forget such minor details and discomfort.

This air-conditioned service area on the autoroute near Lyons gave welcome relief from the 100° F-plus temperatures. It was so intensely hot that the dye from our leathers stained our skin, and the French were walking and driving about in their underwear!

That same exuberance had me on cloud nine the next morning, following the flat, snaking, tree-lined road out of Dijon headed for Switzerland. That seductively sinuous stretch of road is now one of my favourites, and that morning at 8am it was made all the more attractive by the sun breaking through the mist rising from the fields. The haze on the horizon promised searing heat by midday and the road climbed gradually into the Jura foothills. This is hairpin and Armco territory with a vengeance, and if the challenging bends don't take your breath away then the sheer drops into the valleys below certainly will. As the road climbs higher the rare air affects the carburation slightly and the breeze through the pine forests turns refreshingly cooler. It's an ideal riding climate in summer: if you stop to admire the view you soon feel the warmth of the 80-85° sunshine, but on the move it's the nearest you can come to an air-conditioned motorcycle. The higher you go, the bluer the sky, the fresher the air and the sharper the horizons until the road levels out and begins the long descent to Geneva, with Switzerland laid out like a giant carpet before you. At this point I began to realize the drawbacks of travelling alone: there was so much to see and nobody to share the beauty with. At one point I wanted to turn round and say, 'Hey, did you see that!' but I stopped myself just in time. Such sentimentality soon vanished as I concentrated on the downhill stretch, with a seemingly endless succession of steep, blind hairpin bends with the most appalling potholes strategically placed in the best motorcycling line.

There was no time to appreciate the cleanliness and affluence of Geneva as the Yamaha swept back into France for the autoroute to the mouth of the Mont Blanc tunnel. The splendour of the Alps, rising to craggy snow-capped peaks on either side of the road, never fails to impress. No sooner have you spotted a spectacular waterfall spilling gracefully into an abyss half-way up one mountainside on your right than you catch sight of another on your left, higher up and even more breathtaking than the first. Then, out of a sea of tall peaks, you are suddenly confronted by the solid white wall that is Mont Blanc, its majestic broad flanks outlined against a hard blue sky. The temperature is well into the high eighties, but the presence of so much snow has a cooling effect upon the senses.

Through the six-mile dampness of the Mont Blanc tunnel for £1 and I emerged into Italy. The road to the autostrada at Aosta is hewn out of bare rock in places and the stone absorbs the sun's heat, radiating it back at crucifying temperatures. I didn't realize quite how hot it was until I pulled into a service area between Milan and Bologna at 1pm, and the soles of my boots started to melt as they touched the sun-cracked concrete! You find few folk out on the autostrada at midday in summer— just the occasional mad foreign motorcyclist! There was no shade to speak of as I adjusted and lubed the rear chain, chatting to a British rider and his lady on a Guzzi 850—one of only a handful of British motorcyclists I was to see in the whole trip. They were heading back to England, and seemed surprised to hear that I'd left London only the previous morning.

'Where are you headed today?'' asked the Guzzi rider. 'Rome,' I replied, as much for effect as anything else, as I was by no means sure if I would make it. They both looked at me as if I were mad, and said as much. Me, I just basked in my new-found role of hard-riding tourer and headed back out onto the scorched ribbon of tarmac! Some instinct dictated I should call it a day at Florence and cover the remaining distance to Rome at a more leisurely pace the following morning. But stopping would mean paying out for another hotel room and Rome didn't seem all that far away. After all, it was just a matter of sitting there on the Autostrada del Sol and following it into the Eternal City. Darkness fell, and the distant hillsides were lit by numerous forest fires, while the temperature dropped to a more comfortable level and I cruised onwards at a steady 80mph, delighted with the reliability of the 350cc two-stroke and thrilled to bits just to be there, riding.

We rolled into Rome at 11.30pm, the Yam and I, having been in the saddle for 14 hours that day and covering 650 miles. I felt a great sense of achievement at having covered the 1100 miles from London in just two days on the little bike.

It's funny how coincidence follows you wherever you travel. As I queued to pay the final toll near the autostrada exit, I fumbled in my wallet to find the correct notes. The car behind moved position slightly to give me the benefit of its lights, and in my haste to get away again I almost forgot my change. The tale was recounted to my sister at work the next day by the girl behind me in the toll queue, who worked with Barbara and had met me on holiday in Italy the previous summer! Pity I didn't know that at the time she could have saved me a $2\frac{1}{2}$-hour search for the apartment.

That the trip was an enormous success and free from any misfortune— and one of the most enjoyable tours I have ever undertaken—serves to illustrate what is possible with limited experience and using an ordinary everyday motorcycle with no expensive luggage or accessories. The important thing is to be out there on the road, enjoying your motorcycle, seeing new places, hopefully soaking up some good weather, eating good food and generally enjoying a complete change from the daily routine. Doing it is the most important factor; how you do it is purely a matter of detail.

But that's not to say it's not worth spending a little money on accessories or a larger bike to make your trips even more enjoyable. If you can afford to lay your hands on a large-capacity shaft-driven touring bike and fit it out with a good set of quickly detachable motorcycle luggage then the chances are that touring will be more comfortable, less tiring, a lot easier and consequently even more fun. Personal preference plays a big part in making the choice, but in my experience the bigger the bike the better. As a freelance motorcycle journalist I have been lucky enough to ride the majority of bikes on the market; and whenever the arrival of a decent-sized motorcycle could be made to coincide with time off from my full-time work as a non-motorcycling journalist we'd go touring. It would be hard to list them in order of merit, but the machines that made touring easiest and most pleasurable have been any of the 1000cc BMWs, the Honda Gold Wing and CBX, the enormous Z1300 Kawasaki and the XS1100 Yamaha as used by The Bear on his North African tour (see Chapter 8). Now there are plenty of these models about, but we don't see that many out there touring. Part of the reason may be that all of these bikes are among the most expensive you can buy, and some of them are expensive to run, so that proud owners can't afford to use them for their intended purpose. If you'd like to go touring, don't fall into that trap.

Mid-trip maintenance is not one of the highspots of any tour, so regular tourers tend to go for bikes that require little attention on the road. Fortunately the manufacturers have recognized this need in recent years and given us electronic ignition, cast wheels, longer service intervals and, in an increasing number of new models, shaft drive. A bike with shaft final drive has enormous advantages: the rear end stays cleaner, you don't have to carry chain lube and you don't have to get your hands dirty adjusting the chain at the end of a hard day's ride. Having said that, I've included the formidable CBX in my list of favourites because it offers one of the quickest and most exciting ways to cover large distances with ease and comfort. We toured in Ireland on one of the sixes, and enjoyed a thrilling return ride across the north of Wales to cover the 300-plus

My own cross-Channel favourite is the Ramsgate–Calais hovercraft which cuts the sea journey to a mere 35–40 minutes. Conventional ferries take at least 1½ hours

miles from Holyhead to Gravesend in a mere 5 hours 10 minutes. Fuel consumption averaged 40mpg, riding two-up with luggage, and no chain adjustment was required in 1700 miles, although the links were lubed every 300 miles. So if the bike that strikes your fancy seems suitable in every respect but has chain drive you could still find it an excellent touring motorcycle, especially with the latest generation of large, sealed and pre-lubricated chains. Long service intervals are equally important. For example, the 350 Yamaha I took on the Continent needed an oil change every 1500 miles, so this had to be performed by the side of the road in Rome before I could head for home. Fortunately, most of today's new touring bikes can go at least 3000 miles between oil and filter changes, while BMWs can go 5000 and Honda CX500s 7000 miles. It gives you peace of mind and it's one thing less to worry about.

Other factors to consider when choosing your touring bike are comfort of the seat and riding position, engine and exhaust noise levels, vibration, suspension compliance, engine torque, ease of wheel removal in case of punctures and fuel range. Noise can be a real drawback, as we discovered while touring overseas on my own Ducati GT750. This V-twin is a great touring mount, with superb handling and a long-legged loping gait, but with the standard Conti megaphones (silencers would be an inappropriate term) the exhaust noise gets annoying after a few hundred miles. Fuel range is a highly contentious subject, as manufacturers in the sixties and seventies persisted in fitting even the largest fuel guzzlers with ridiculously small fuel tanks. Things started to improve in 1979, but you still need to be careful. Most touring riders know only too well the annoyance of having to stop for fuel every 130 miles and then spending the next half-hour catching up with all the cars, coaches and trucks that had previously been left behind miles back.

This problem was particularly galling on that first trip of mine aboard the two-stroke Yamaha, which returned 40mpg and had a tank capacity of less than $2\frac{1}{2}$ gallons. This meant that fuel stops were about $1\frac{1}{2}$ hours apart, and on a 14-hour ride that adds up to a lot of wasted time. A further problem arose in Italy with the Government-issued petrol coupons, which cut the cost of petrol to tourists by a third. They were issued in 10-litre units, and my tank held just over 10 litres, which meant that I had to run almost dry to get full value from the coupons; no change could be given. At one stage on the autostrada the engine showed signs of running out of fuel after many miles on reserve, but just then I crested a rise and there, half a mile away, was a service area; the engine died and I coasted to a halt three yards from the petrol pumps! Talk about the luck of the Irish. . . .

The same luck held out years later when my wife and I were riding my Yamaha XS750 northwards along the autostrada on the west coast of Italy near Genoa, heading for the south of France. We had just got over the annoyance of discovering at the last petrol stop that our few remaining pre-paid petrol coupons had blown away in the wind from my un-zipped jacket pocket—a simple but careless mistake. The Yamaha triple had just run on to reserve again when we saw a sign for the next Area di

Servizio, 30km distant. Past experience showed that the Yamaha could manage 24 miles on reserve, but no more, so the 30km should prove no problem. A series of marker boards announced the impending presence of the service area: 20km, 10km, 7km, 3km, 1km. There was a service area there all right—or rather there would be in about six months' time when they'd finished building it! There was nothing we could do but ride on, even more slowly, in the intense heat. The 24 reserve miles came and went without any sign of a filling station, and we grew increasingly concerned about the prospect of running dry in one of the many long, dark tunnels where the motorway runs straight through the hillside. Such is the contrast between the bright sunlight and the blackness of the tunnels that anyone stopping in there stood a very good chance of being run down by a speeding Fiat. With speed now down to 50mph and 29.5 miles after switching to reserve we finally rolled into the most welcome service area it has been my misfortune to frequent!

Having taken all these factors into consideration, compiled a short-list, read all the road tests you can get hold of and chosen your touring bike, there's the question of luggage and accessories. The most basic necessity is probably a good tank bag: they're not very expensive, are an ideal way of carrying quite a lot of gear, will not damage your paintwork if handled with care, and suffer only the slight drawback of making petrol stops just that little bit more complicated. The next most useful item is a luggage rack, although this should never be used to carry too much heavy baggage as that can seriously affect your machine's handling. It's best to pick a rack that will suit the panniers (saddlebags to non-Anglo-Saxons) you may eventually want to buy. Panniers range from inexpensive soft throwover types that work remarkably well and are very convenient, to highly expensive lockable and quickly detachable suitcase-style models that look at home in the very best hotels. It's basically a question of money: pay enough and you can have your luggage colour-coded for your bike. If money isn't too much of a problem and you're going to do a lot of touring and like to have high-quality equipment then you should be looking at the panniers made by firms such as Krauser, BMW, Samsonite, Sigma, Craven and Vetter.

Whether or not to fit a fairing is a purely personal consideration. Some riders love them, others don't. The Bear, for example, swears by his fairing and even fitted his XL250 Honda with a windshield. But on all but the coldest and wettest days (when I try to arrange *not* to be touring) I prefer the feel of a naked machine. For me, a fairing only adds to the engine noise and acts like a sail, either being pushed or pulled by the wind. Good fairings are not cheap, so the best bet is to try touring on an unfaired motorcycle and then, if you find it too uncomfortable or you're just plain curious, think about adding a fairing next time out. Once you have the bike and equipment sorted out to the mutual satisfaction of yourself and your bank manager, actually getting out there to go touring farther afield is fairly straightforward these days. Let's look at getting out of Britain and roaming around the Continent.

The English Channel is criss-crossed by a multitude of car ferry routes but, as befits the world's busiest waterway, it's also one of the most expensive stretches of water to cross. I guess I am lucky to live less than an hour's ride from the nearest port, so I always prefer to make an early start and catch a 7am ferry to make the most of that first day's riding in France. I also like to get the ferry trip over with as quickly as possible, so I prefer to go by hovercraft from Ramsgate to Calais. This service is operated by Hoverlloyd, takes 30 to 40 minutes depending on the weather and costs no more than a normal ferry boat at about £50 return for bike and two riders. Ramsgate has the added advantage that most of the holiday traffic branches off to Dover, and this leaves a relatively clear run into the hoverport. Hoverlloyd will take only two motorcycles at a time, due to lack of space, but you can book your passage in advance. I find it an eminently civilized way of starting and finishing any continental touring holiday, with none of the delays that invariably seem to hit conventional ferries.

Harmonization of legislation on either side of the Channel means that you can now turn up unannounced at a ferry port, pay your fare and disembark in France without making any arrangements or complying with any formalities beyond a simple passport check before departure. A full UK driving licence is valid throughout Europe and a UK insurance policy gives you minimum legal cover in all the EEC countries plus a few others, including Switzerland. But it is worthwhile extending your full UK cover to all the countries you plan to visit, insuring your belongings and obtaining an Italian translation of your driving licence from the AA or RAC if you plan to visit Italy. You should also take the bike's registration document and, if it's not your own machine, a letter authorizing you to use the bike. Travellers' cheques are a good safe way of carrying your funds, but it's also wise to take some currency for each of the countries you intend to visit. It's not unknown for the bureau de change at the border to be closed when you pass through, or, if it's open, for there to be large queues in high season.

Things don't always work out as you've planned though: on one trip I arrived at the hoverport to discover that the one thing I'd forgotten was my driving licence. We pressed on, aware that if anything did go wrong on the other side I'd have some explaining to do. Then, last time out, I made a mental note to take all the necessary documentation with me—only to have my wallet stolen the day before we set off, complete with driving licence, insurance certificate and credit card! Sometimes you can't win. . . .

France is a country you either love or hate. If your destination is some distant land then you want to get as many French miles under your wheels as possible that first day. But taken as a destination in itself, France has a great deal to offer. Paris is an obvious attraction, for who can resist the pleasures of sipping coffee at a pavement café in the Champs-Élysées or Montmartre watching an elegant world float past. The Louvre, the Eiffel Tower, the Arc de Triomphe, Notre Dame and the Place de la Concorde are all good reasons to stop; the prices, the traffic and the tourists are all good reasons to leave. There's nothing interesting about the area immediately surrounding the French Channel ports, except perhaps the thought-provoking sight of so many graves from two world wars. But as you get deeper into France you start to notice the changes in architecture. There are a great many new and comfortable-looking houses not far from the main roads, but they're invariably surrounded by dry, sandy soil and possibly a vegetable garden; lush green lawns and cared-for flower beds are rare, giving the houses a strangely part-finished look that is typically rural French. The roads are generally quiet away from the ports, with the expensive autoroutes accommodating the holiday traffic.

You don't have to get too deeply into France to find picturesque scenery and get away from the masses. The wine-producing region around the old cathedral city of Reims is one area offering plenty to do and see. Reims itself is unremarkable except for its eleventh-century cathedral, but it is the centre of the Champagne Belt, with most of the major producers based nearby at Epernay. You can visit the various famous champagne houses and have a guided tour of miles of underground tunnels and caves where millions of bottles of bubbly are stored at a constant 50°F, and then enjoy a free glass of the magic brew before you go. Last year we bought a bottle of 1978 Moët et Chandon and consumed its contents with French bread, spring onions and cream cheese in a peaceful suntrap by the roadside. Now that is really living! We even had to resort to buying two tubs of ice-cream so we could use the empty cartons as glasses!

That was a particularly pleasant and relaxed trip, but it is also memorable as the one occasion when we split up with our travelling companions. Coupled with the experiences of The Bear in Chapter 9 it serves as a cautionary tale in choosing touring partners. Ray and Anne were among our best friends of more than five years' standing. Ray was a keen tourer within Britain and had just ventured farther afield for the first time the previous year, taking his son to Milan on his CX500. Anne had enjoyed brief spins locally on the pillion, but had never gone touring. At first we had planned to spend two weeks riding from New York to Los Angeles, but later ruled this out for a variety of reasons—chiefly cost. We then toyed with going to the Cotswolds, but eventually opted for a long weekend in the Champagne district of France. We realized immediately that we were far from ideal travelling companions, despite our close friendship: Ray liked to ride slowly, I prefer to ride fast; they liked to stop and look at buildings and areas of architectural or historic interest, we're more used to 500-mile days and areas of natural beauty. In any event we set off in good spirits and had a thoroughly enjoyable time for the first two days, although I admit to having to suppress some frustration at continually waiting for the others to catch up, despite cruising at 55mph. But we'd agreed to make the entire tour at their pace, so we pottered.

Tempers flared the third day out, though. Chris was getting tetchy with me for trying to up the pace every now and then; Ray kept worrying about going over our daily budget for accommodation and meals; we didn't always agree on where to stop or where to eat and finally Anne

The spectacular beauty of the Amalfi Drive is a must for every touring rider with a head for heights. We cut inland here and 20 minutes later were still in the same spot—but a few thousand feet higher!

decided that if everything didn't happen according to her plan we should go our separate ways. There was no changing her mind, so the two groups returned home the same way—but separately, an hour or so apart. Before we set out I wouldn't have believed it could happen, but now that I know it can and does happen I would advise anyone to think seriously about who they go touring with. It didn't matter much, in practical terms, on a short trip to France, but imagine the effect if the same thing had occurred half-way across America and one party was dependent on the other for tools, camping equipment or vital spares. No, I reckon it's safer to have your own holiday and risk losing your friends by boring them to death with a blow-by-blow account afterwards!

Fortunately, camping equipment was not a problem on this trip. We prefer to stay in small hotels for comfort and convenience, but most of continental Europe is blessed with excellent campsites. Facilities generally include launderettes, hot showers, shops and in some cases even a heated swimming pool. Prices range from £2.50 to £4 a night— not far short of the price of a clean room in a small hotel. If you're staying in hotels you need to start looking by 5pm at the latest. Looking for a hotel—now there's a task! I remember on my way home from that first visit to Italy I rolled into the town of Aosta in the Italian Alps and pulled up at the first hotel I saw, the Vallee d'Aosta, at about 5.15 in the afternoon. The receptionist looked down his nose at my travel-stained figure and said 'Tout complet'. The same happened in the next four hotels I tried, and I was beginning to get desperate when the propietor of the Hotel Carla offered me a room with dinner and breakfast for £6. I was as tight as Scrooge in those days and thought that was a bit steep. I toyed with the idea of pressing on across the Alps to Geneva in the hope of finding a cheaper room there, but wondered about the sanity of riding those lethal roads in the gathering dusk. So I phoned my sister back in Rome and asked her if she thought *le patron* was trying to pull a fast one. Her reply was uncharacteristically straightforward: 'It's a bargain! Get back there and take it before someone else does!' If I hadn't taken her advice I'd have missed the pleasure of waking up to an awe-inspiring view of the snow-covered Alps at sunrise—at no extra cost! But more importantly, I'd have missed one of the most amazing conversations of my lifetime. At dinner that evening—an excellent meal, by the way— I shared a table with a Venezuelan electrician who was just passing through. He spoke no English, I knew about ten words of Italian, and we both spoke a little French, but by combining the spoken word with gesticulations and moving knives, forks and glasses around the table we spent an hour talking motorcycles. He used to scramble a Ducati 450 in South American motocross events until he broke his arm badly and his Italian wife made him give up for good! It's good to know that the problems of marriage and motorcycling are universal!

Three years later, when I convinced my wife Chris that the best way of spending two weeks in the summer was to ride down to Amalfi, south of Naples, she agreed on one condition: that we would pre-book into good hotels for the first couple of days on the road. At least she could ease into Continental touring without the additional worry of where we'd rest our heads for the night. 'I don't mind how many miles we cover in the day as long as we can get a good night's sleep,' was her reasoning. The only trouble is that British travel agents are not keen to book one-night stands in Continental hotels for their customers. We persuaded the agent that arranges all travel for the company I worked for at the time to book us into four-star hotels in Dijon and Aosta at a cost of roughly £20 a night at 1978 prices. An added benefit is that you've been home a month after the trip before you get billed! We couldn't afford that sort of luxury for more than a couple of nights, but it was worth every penny to have comfortable bathrooms *en suite* in which we could soak away the dirt and aches of a 500-mile day before relaxing over a couple of steaks and a bottle of good wine. Unfortunately Continental plumbing is not renowned for its efficiency and on those first two nights we managed to soak away rather more than the road dirt! In Dijon Chris had a bath while I unpacked our panniers. When I went into the bathroom she had already pulled the plug on the bath and was standing on a clean white bath mat in the middle of the floor towelling herself dry. Even as I watched, a damp patch appeared in the centre of the mat and spread slowly outwards. The expanding ring of water seemed to bear no relationship to anything else going on in the room—until I pulled the mat away to reveal a drain in the middle of the floor through which the old bathwater was slowly rising!

Mopping-up operations were resumed the following evening, when I took a shower at the Hotel Vallee d'Aosta. Now some Continental showers are a little on the small side and this one was no exception. If the shower curtain was left to hang inside the shower base there just wasn't enough room for any serious washing, so I let it hang outside instead. About ten minutes later I emerged to find the bathroom under about an inch of water, which was moving slowly across the tiles towards the bedroom door—and the thick carpet of the corridor! The chambermaids next morning must have thought we'd spent the night having baths, because I grabbed every towel in the room to stem the flood and mop up the mess, finishing just in time for a waiter to arrive with some drinks we'd ordered. This was the same hotel that had turned me away in 1975 and I couldn't help feeling a touch of smugness as we sat down in the very comfortable dining room and tucked into a glorious Châteaubriand and a bottle of Valpolicella. Generally, though, motorcyclists on the Continent are treated as civilized beings and are not barred from bars, restaurants or hotels because of their mode of transport. Mind you, I have never been refused service in Britain or Ireland as a motorcyclist, but tales of discrimination are legion, in England especially.

The continentals seem so well disposed towards motorcycles. When we left Dijon that summer for Aosta we hit our first traffic jam of the trip just where the road branched off near Chamonix for the Mont Blanc tunnel. It was only midday and our hotel was barely an hour's ride away if we chose to travel through the tunnel, so instead we decided to head back into Switzerland and take the Great St Bernard pass into Italy. Half a mile up the road in the picturesque skiing village of Chamonix we saw the cause of the jam. The village square was cordoned off into one great paddock into which was squeezed an amazing array of modern motorcycles and vintage and classic cars. We'd stumbled across the annual vintage car tour around Mont Blanc. At irregular intervals magnificent old cars would bellow and snort their way out on to the main street, their drivers resplendent in immaculate white overalls and even a white leather flying helmet in one instance! The marshals for the event were motorcyclists on all manner of customized machines. There was a Suzuki GS550 with Campagnola magnesium wheels, Ace bars and a white leather seat! Over to one side someone was starting up a pink Harley, while helmetless marshals rocketed away on Guzzi Le Mans and Egli Kawasakis. A gendarme waved us on, too, from the head of the traffic queue, even though more than half the cars had still to join the run.

I let the Yamaha growl in pursuit of the first group and quickly

More than 2000 miles into the trip and the XS750 is still spotless at Amalfi

overhauled the pink Harley and an old M20 sidecar outfit. As we moved out of town we tucked in behind a rorty old Morgan three-wheeler, pausing to watch the occupants' weird cornering technique before shooting past. The road was lined with hordes of children; it looked as if the entire population of the region had come out to watch the amazing spectacle. We were regarded as legitimate participants, since everyone waved us through just as vigorously as they did the bona fide entrants and marshals. A couple of Kawasakis in café racer trim rocketed past and vanished around the next series of bends as we came up behind a strange old four-wheeler. It obviously had a rigid rear axle and no differential, and the passenger was energetic in his efforts to lean out of either side in a bid to get the contraption around corners. Then we passed the big red open car with its leather-helmeted crew and a large, low old sports car which glued itself to our tail and manged to stay with us until we reached the Swiss border, where all the rally entrants were stopped while we were waved through.

The road climbed the mountain ahead and we stopped for lunch on the terrace of a restaurant several hundred feet above the white city of Martigny. While we gorged ourselves on vast ham and salami open sandwiches in the midday sun we were entertained by a mobile display of vintage and modern machinery as the rally cars and their two-wheeled escort roared down the mountainside past the restaurant in an orgy of colour and sound. This unscheduled entertainment had slowed our progress. It was getting late, so we skipped the Great St Bernard pass and instead settled for the welcome cool of the more convenient tunnel of the same name. One side of the approach to the tunnel is open on the right and flanked by a series of pillars, which give a magnificent view of the mountains and a large glistening lake that nestles among them.

The Italian customs post is situated in the tunnel itself, and we stopped to find a young customs official eager to check our passports. Chris handed them over, and the Italian's eyes lit up when he found himself holding one British document and one Irish. He held them aloft, one in each hand. 'Ah, British, Irish; fight, fight, fight, yes?' he beamed, waving the passports around in the air. We assured him we always got along just fine, so his mind explored new possibilities. 'Eh, one Catholic, one Protestant; fight, fight, yes?' We assured him of our religious harmony and, happy in the knowledge that we were both Roman Catholic, he handed back our respective blue and green passports and wished us a pleasant stay in Italy. The whole hilarious incident ended with his superior officer giving him a filthy look for such frivolity!

The Italian temperament is one of the nicest things about touring in Italy, but it's also one of the drawbacks. If you're not in a vast hurry their easy-going, almost careless attitude to life has tremendous appeal for work-weary refugees from the seriousness of London or Bonn. But if you want anything done quickly and efficiently the whole system seems to work against you and can drive impatient people right up the wall. You can queue for an hour in a busy Rome bank to cash a travellers' cheque while half a dozen male cashiers chat up some raven-haired beauty at the far end of the counter; or sit around for three hours in the middle of the day waiting for a petrol station to open after the siesta; or get run down by a gaggle of Fiats going the wrong way down a one-way street in Naples; or be trampled under the feet of some of the rudest people in Europe as they literally fight for a seat on a bus or train. Where else would they decide to solve the problems caused by a long Post Office strike by burning the backlog of mail?

The joy of Italy is that there's so much to compensate for the idiosyncracies of the natives. The weather in summer is invariably hot, dry and sunny. The food is exceptional, even in service areas on the autostrada, where two people can eat large helpings of lasagne, fresh rolls, desert and local wine for less than £6. Try that in Britain! Pasta with bread and house wine in infinite combinations make every meal a satisfying gastronomic adventure, ringing the changes with pizza, salad and veal when the spaghetti starts coming out of your ears. Italy is still one of the cheapest places in Europe to eat out. The architecture is something else. From the Ponte Vecchio and the golden doors of the baptistry in Florence, through the familiar sights of St Peter's, the Forum, the Colosseum and the Victor Emmanuel monument in Rome to the ancient splendour of the ruins of Pompeii, there is enough variety to capture the imagination

Arch-enthusiasts Geoff and Jenny Wilson from Cumbria in the north of England don't like making things too easy; they spent Christmas touring Finland in sub-zero temperatures on this Honda 900/Squire sidecar combination

of any traveller. Throw in the treasures of the Vatican museum, the spectacular ceiling of the Sistine Chapel, the eerie Catacombs and the old and worn Appian Way and you can be sure of plenty to do and see every day. The language isn't too hard to cope with, but it can lead one into unexpected difficulties. Friends touring on a Honda CB500 in Florence came across a sign pointing to 'Senso Unico'. It was only after following the directions for ages and literally running around in circles that it dawned on them that the sign was not to guide tourists towards some 'unique sight' but was merely to indicate a one-way street!

Sun can also play tricks with the unwary visitor to Italy. On our second day in Rome we set off for the beach at Ostia on the 750 Yamaha—a trip of only 30 miles—and took great care on the beach not to get sunburned first day out. Riding home again at about 5 o'clock in the afternoon, clad only in tee-shirt, shorts and sandles, I felt the heat of the strong sun burning into my skin every time we stopped. It was almost unbearable, but there was nothing for it but to carry on. The trip lasted only 55 minutes, but by that time the damage was done. We were both out of circulation for the next two days with severe and very painful sunburn. My left ankle had received the full treatment and became purple and swollen, leaving me hobbling about in agony until various medications had eased the misery. It was a salutary lesson which we did well to bear in mind later in the week. We had ridden up into the hills outside Rome to trundle slowly through the town of Frascati and the picturesque village of Rocca di Papa and on to Castel Gandolfo. There we posed for photographs outside the Pope's summer palace at the end of the main street, little realizing that a week later Pope Paul VI was to die within its walls. The palace overlooks a large lake, and in the heat our thoughts turned again to swimming, so we headed back towards the coast with the intention of stopping at one of the public pay beaches we'd used before.

We got as far as Castel Fusano when we saw a long stretch of golden sand dunes and a walkway leading from the road. The sand looked cleaner than on the pay beaches, and this one was free, so we marched onto the beach. It was quiet by Ostia standards, both in volume of noise and volume of people. Chris noticed it first. She thought she was seeing things, but a glance up the golden sands showed we were surrounded by nude men. For a second we thought we were on a gay beach, but then I saw we were also surrounded by nude women—walking about, sunbathing, swimming, playing badminton. About half the sunbathers wore swimming trunks or bikinis, and a number of women were topless, but everyone else was starkers. It's funny how quickly you can get used to the idea, so we stayed put and enjoyed the scenery, with me especially taking care not to get burned where the sun never shines! A couple of things stood out. One was the way everybody looked so nonchalant about stripping, as if they'd been doing this sort of thing for years—only the white patches showed they hadn't been doing it for long! The other was the inherent vanity of Italian men. One guy was standing on top of a sand dune, naked, turning himself round a few degrees every ten minutes

43

The original stones laid in Roman times are still visible in parts of the Via Appia Antica in Rome. It is lined by monuments to the rich and noble families of ancient Rome

or so to get an even all-over tan. Then there was this teenager who went swimming with his trunks on, got out a few yards away from us and a couple of basking beauties, then calmly took off his trunks and wandered off slowly, smiling. That's Italians for you!

If they're not strutting around on beaches they're busy making an art form out of driving badly—no, make that atrociously. When we hit Naples we came upon a two-way street designed to take two lanes of cars in each direction, with a solid white line down the middle. But because the volume of traffic going south was by far the greater, the drivers took it upon themselves to use all four lanes in one direction. A thin line of Fiat 500s tried to squeeze northwards between the other cars and the pavement; then some of them started driving on the pavement as well. What the southbound drivers had all forgotten was that this street also had tram tracks running up the centre, so, when two trams tried to force their way up against the tide of Neapolitan madness, chaos reigned supreme. More cars took to the pavements; the others tried to split in the middle to let the trams by. It was the ultimate traffic mess. When we eventually fought our way out of it we had to ride for 20 minutes through the most depressing slums I have ever encountered, along garbage-strewn cobbled streets wet with overflowing drains in the 95° heat. After paying a 500-lire toll to get in we had to cough up a further 100 lire to get out! 'See Naples and die'—we know what you mean.

Seeking relief at the ruins of Pompeii only brought more Neapolitan traits to the fore: an enterprising ice-cream salesman tried to charge us 1600 lire (about £1 or $2.00) to have his son 'look after' the Yamaha and our two helmets while we went sightseeing. We parked the bike on the pavement for free and tipped the official museum cloakroom attendant 300 lire to take charge of our gear. After two hot and sweaty hours exploring the ruins, with their well-preserved murals and lava-encrusted bodies, we rode down to Vietri and the beginning of the Amalfi Drive. This is a narrow and hair-raising little road that hugs the cliff edge along the rugged Amalfi coastline for miles, several hundred feet above the sea. While enjoying the delights of one of the most dangerous stretches of motorcycling road anywhere we were surprised to be flagged down by a fat, uniformed little man who came running from a building by the roadside. I slowed, ready to stop, not sure whether he was a policeman. It turned out that he was touting us to take a room in his 'very nice, very clean' hotel! Italians!

Those are the really funny and memorable parts of any trip, though; they're as natural in Italy as unisex toilets in France, queues in England, chatty strangers in Ireland or the ubiquitous 'have a nice day' in America. If you don't like it you'd better stay at home. If you keep an open mind and accept these national eccentricities as part of the fun of travelling in general and touring in particular, then Europe provides some marvellous contrasts. You can experience them to the full in the space of a normal two-week vacation: the sunshine of Spain and Portugal, the cuisine and topless beaches of the south of France, the beauty of the Rhine Valley, the splendour of the Alps, the romanticism of Italy or the

The Yamaha drew a lot of attention from the package-tour crowds in the coaches. Riding in Rome traffic is pretty hair-raising at first but you soon get used to the foibles of the Italians

picturesque coastal scenery of Yugoslavia. To get the best out of places farther afield, such as Greece and Turkey, it is necessary to add a week to your schedule unless you aim to spend most of your time in the saddle. And the whole holiday can work out a darned sight cheaper by bike than the dubious pleasure of a two-week package deal in the appalling mediocrity of Benidorm.

The funny thing about touring in Europe is that I've yet to meet any motorcyclist who has tried it once and not wanted to go back again and again. There's enough variety out there to keep the most ardent tourer happy for several years. And if that isn't enough to satisfy your particular brand of wanderlust then maybe—just maybe—you're ready to follow in the tracks of The Bear for The Big Trip.

Chapter 3

'Why don't we go to see the Guinness brewery?'

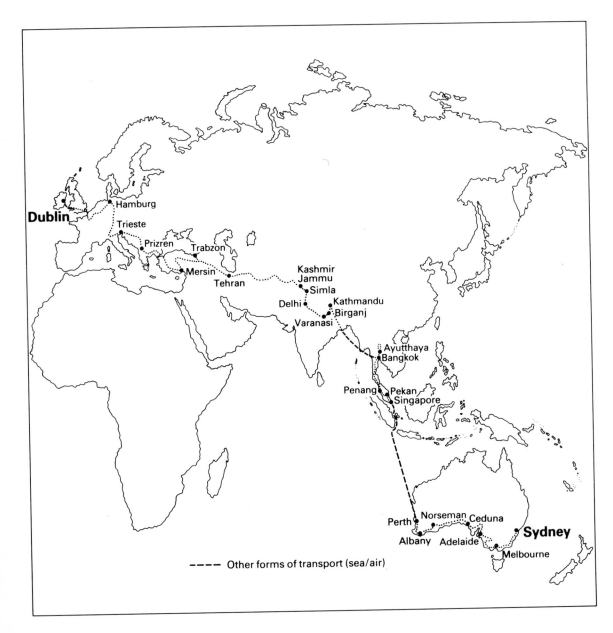

Dublin · Hamburg · Trieste · Prizren · Trabzon · Mersin · Tehran · Kashmir · Jammu · Simla · Delhi · Kathmandu · Birganj · Varanasi · Ayutthaya · Bangkok · Penang · Pekan · Singapore · Perth · Norseman · Ceduna · Albany · Adelaide · Melbourne · Sydney

- - - - Other forms of transport (sea/air)

Sydney to Singapore

CHARLIE AND I were comfortable: with generous glasses of Glenfiddich in our hands, we were lying back in overstuffed armchairs in Charlie's living-room in Sydney. It was very late, the party had been over for quite a while, and we were talking in the desultory way you do at such times. Both of us were at loose ends. Charlie had nearly finished his thesis for a PhD in botany, disclosing the private life of an obscure little wild flower; I was heartily sick of working in an advertising agency. The talk revolved around alternatives, our bikes, booze . . . and suddenly it all came together in my mind.

'Why don't we ride over to Ireland and visit the Guinness brewery?'

Our touring experience at this stage was fairly limited. Charlie had covered some amazing distances on his old Honda XL250, true, but it had been rallying rather than touring. My long-distance runs had been to get somewhere: opening the old WLA Harley up and pointing it at Melbourne, or perhaps my mother's place in Ballina, hardly counts as touring. Although there had been one memorable trip. . . .

My friend Campbell owned an eleven-year-old BMW R60 and we were going to the Intervarsity Jazz Convention in Armidale on it. Seeing that we had a bit of extra time, we thought we'd have a look at Queensland on the way. The first few hundred miles went quite well despite persistent overheating. On the north coast of New South Wales we had our first flat tyre: the tube was butyl, but we didn't know that and fixed it the way you would a rubber one. Naturally, the patch came off again: flat tyre No. 2. We bought a new tube, but could only get one that was slightly too small: that lasted a day. The next tube was the right size, but by now the tyre was so badly split that it chewed the new tube up. Eleven flat tyres, three new tubes and one tyre in three days, not to mention the steamroller that nearly ran the bike over in Yeppoon.

It wasn't all like that, of course. We had some marvellous times in the little pubs and enjoyed the scenery and the riding. We enjoyed the jazz, too, when we finally made it to Armidale—but not the ride home; the bike had lost an enormous amount of power. When Campbell stripped it down after our return it wasn't hard to see why. There were hardly any rings left: that overheating must have done a bit of damage. Not exactly the most brilliant background for a bike tour around the world. We had decided that we might as well go on around the world, coming home via America. After all, once the bikes were loaded up. . . .

The choice of bikes wasn't difficult once we sat down and listed our requirements. We wanted singles, for simplicity and lightness: a single is easier to look after, to tune and to repair on the road, and when you have to ship the bike, be it by air or sea, the lighter it is the cheaper it is. Trail bikes, dual-purpose on-off road machines, seemed indicated for ruggedness. Some of the roads in Asia, and not only in Asia, don't deserve the name and road bikes can be a little flimsy. In addition, trail bikes cope with mud and rivers much better.

The bikes would have to be Japanese. It's bad enough trying to buy spares for fairly common bikes, but just imagine trying to find a clutch cable for a Malaguti in Rawalpindi! Neither of us liked two-strokes so the choice was simple—XT500s or XL250s. These days the choice is much wider, but at the beginning of 1978 the only other four-stroke trail bikes around were tiddlers. I wasn't about to attempt the Afghani desert on a 125, so we settled for XLs, because Charlie already had one. I had little trouble finding another in good condition and at a reasonable price. Our friendly bike shop stripped the bikes down and checked them over: both bikes were found to have worn camshafts, and these were replaced, unnecessarily, as it turned out. Apparently XL camshafts wear to a certain point and then wear no further.

We bought some plastic panniers that looked reasonably waterproof. Jim Traeger, a friend of mine and a biker from way back, made up strong cage-style carriers for them. These would double as crash bars, and they also carried one-gallon containers, one for spare fuel and one for water. Plastic enduro tanks replaced the tiny metal ones and we fitted larger rear sprockets for easier cruising and had some aluminium tank boxes made up. These had holes cut out of their bases which fitted over the filler holes in the tanks and were secured by the petrol cap. It meant unpacking them every time we filled up with petrol, but with the lids of the boxes locked, the tanks were effectively locked also. Unfortunately the electrical system of the XL won't support better lights and air horns, so we had to make do with the inadequate originals.

Then came the hard decisions. What to take? We packed a large and comprehensive first-aid box containing antihistamines, antibiotics and pills against malaria and stomach bugs, antiseptic, burn creams and bandages. Spares for the bikes filled half a pannier; they included cables, bulbs, electrical bits and pieces, chains, liquid gasket and WD40. Our toolkits were augmented by a set of sockets and an impact driver.

We would take a tent and camp until Perth, then send the tent back and use hotels and hostels for the rest of the trip. We bought wet weather gear, yachting clothes in my case, because I wanted the stuff to be light. Charlie bought heavyweight working gear: he was right, of course. His gear lasted the whole trip; mine failed me rather badly. The bikes were finished in time for our departure, but only just. It is truly amazing just what can turn up to delay you, but we *were* ready when the first guests for our farewell party arrived. The bikes were all packed and lined up outside the front door. I will draw a considerate curtain of silence over the abominable acts performed by members of the Sydney University

Motorcycle Club that night. When the time came for us to leave, I had had half an hour of sleep, Charlie had had none and the guard of honour to see us off had shrunk from 40 to one. The entire club, barring only one intrepid soul, was asleep.

So were we, not long after departure. Our route took us through the Royal National Park south of Sydney, and we took advantage of a shady river bank to catch a bit of shut-eye: we'd done all of 30km so far. The afternoon saw us a little further along our way, but the weather was already demonstrating some of the nastiness it would be handing out later on. By the time we had passed Wollongong, some 80km from Sydney, a cloudburst had caught us. Its relatives followed us for the rest of the day as we rolled south on Highway 1. We found a river cave to sleep in that first night, with a pool in front, but we left some of our clothes under a drip from the stone ceiling. A lot to learn, yet.

Julie and Trevor, friends of Charlie's, sheltered us the next night and tried to teach us mah-jong into the bargain. Then we sat out on the verandah, looking out over their little bit of the Ranges, and had a few quiet drinks. Trevor, who is quite a brilliant mechanic, brazed up some braces for the back of our pannier racks the next day. His workshop was across the road from McConkey's pub—'The Killarney of the South'—so we ducked over there for a Guinness with lunch. They were out of Guinness.

We played boy motocross racers on some of the mud roads along the coast, and Charlie's Trials Universals beat my Avon Roadrunners every time. Not being much of a dirt rider, I was petrified. Back on the tar, we rolled down through the state forests that straddle the border ranges, still in the rain, of course. But it's so peaceful down there, ridge after ridge of forest rolling away to the horizon.

In southern Victoria, 600 miles into the trip, we're about to tackle the Great Ocean Road—one of Australia's great bike roads

Lakes Entrance provided fresh scallops from the local Fishermen's Coop, and I fried them in butter for a memorable meal. Lunch the next day was marine again, the Yarram Hotel turning out a seafood platter for $3 that consisted of grilled fish, deep-fried battered scallops, oysters and prawns with an excellent salad. Australian pub lunches can be superb.

Gippsland's straight roads took us further south, to Wilson's Promontory. This is a national park and the Department of National Parks and Wildlife (hereinafter, if ever again, referred to as PAW) make absolutely sure you don't forget it. There are more signs than plants in the otherwise lovely, rugged, stony park. We camped at Tidal River among the black, dripping ti-trees and drank quantities of bourbon and milk. For medicinal purposes only.

Friends put us up in Melbourne, and we spent a great deal of time in the excellent Chinese and Greek restaurants that city has to offer. As a Sydney-sider, I am obliged to add at this stage that Melbourne doesn't have a great deal *else* to offer ... we take our intercapital rivalries seriously. There being a shortage of helmets, we got around by car. 'Err ... this car has a bullet hole in the door.' Gaby, the proud owner, nodded. Apparently she had been driving along out in the country one night when there was a bang. When she got home, she extracted a .303 bullet from the padding in her seat. My friend Lee grinned, 'Who said Australia isn't the frontier any more, eh?' she asked.

The Geelong freeway took us out of town a couple of days later and no one shot at us. We took the Great Ocean Road west along the coast, throwing the poor little XLs around as if they were Dukes. This is a marvellous bike road with twists and turns along the cliffs and a reasonable surface. Lunch was at Lorne, in a pub that reminded me of the Grand at Brighton, then we were ready for the dirt and gravel surface after Apollo Bay.

There's no problem about finding a campsite in the Nullarbor Plain—1000 miles of semi-desert

Down to our campsite at the Red Johanna, the gravel was deep enough to swallow a bike whole, but we survived to sit on the clifftop and watch the sea mist roll in and envelop the coast in gauze. The next day took us through equal parts of state forest and grazing land to Mt Gambier with its famous Blue Lake, where every year it seems to claim one or two skindivers looking for its mysterious water supply. We had a very Australian dinner at Mac's Hotel, the local cocky's pub. Cockies are farmers, not cockatoos (although that seems to be where the name comes from), and you can have cow cockies, wheat cockies or sheep cockies. They all eat and drink well, as we found out.

The Coorong, a seaside desert rather strangely full of waterways, kept us amused the next day as we tried out its numerous little sand-tracks. We needed the rest by the time we found a campsite on the shores of Lake Albert; I wonder what makes my body think that hanging onto the handlebars *really* hard will stop the bike from falling over? It doesn't work, you know. We left the pelicans nodding sagely on the lake the next morning and made our way up past Bordertown to Tailem Bend. Our first sight of the Murray River gave us not only a view of the longest river system on the continent but also of the *Murray Queen*, one of the last paddle steamers plying it. Very majestic she looked, too.

The run into Adelaide was a bit grim on the new ridgetop motorway, which was exposed to the scorching desert winds. We had lunch at Hahndorf, in the German Arms pub; there's a large expatriate German community down here and they haven't forgotten how to cook decent schnitzel. The Adelaide Hills provided a last bit of riding amusement before we rolled into the South Australian capital, dry and tired. Once again we had friends to put us up and put up with us, and Adelaide provided its famous Arts Festival for our amusement. Then the road took us towards the Flinders Range, and we registered our best petrol-consumption figures for the trip: 77mpg, but we did have a tailwind. Not far out of Adelaide we thought the end of the trip had come rather early as we rolled into a little town called—Dublin! We camped that night in Germein Gorge in the Flinders and had to be very careful with our fire—everything was dry; even the creek had long since ceased to flow. We were carrying our own water, of course.

At Pookara, we turned off Highway 1 to go down to Streaky Bay. The campsite was rather uninspiring, although the bay itself looked good with its alternating light and dark sea floor. We did find some inspiration that night in the pub, watching a little blonde, who was dancing in the tightest gold lamé pants I have ever seen. Nothing was open the next morning, and breakfast had to wait until we reached Smoky Bay, where the General Store provided some geriatric biscuits. It's grim country down there, but the people are friendly; Ceduna was pleasant enough, more like a suburb of Sydney than a town on the edge of the Nullarbor Plain. There we met a bloke who was touring the country in a converted bus. As a runabout, he carried a Kawasaki 1000 in the back—complete with sidecar.

Outside Penong there was a forest of windmills all mounted on wheeled trolleys— another testament to the inhospitability of the land. It wasn't much farther to the 'Nullarbor—treeless plain' sign, where we saw our first wombat of the trip—he was just trundling along minding his own business, and disappeared before I could get the camera out. Nullarbor, by the way, is from the Latin and just means 'no trees'. That's quite accurate, too. The road is mostly straight and not very interesting, unless you find flat ground with occasional small, dried-out bushes interesting. There are signs warning of camels crossing the road, but we didn't see any of the actual animals. Camels were imported into Australia to carry supplies out to work parties in the desert and have multiplied in the wild.

To make camp, we went half a mile or so off the road and found ourselves a little sheltered hollow. There was plenty of small timber for a fire, and the stars looked the way they only ever do in the desert: cold, small and piercingly bright. There are twice as many out there as anywhere else.

When we finally reached the coast the next day, we found a slip road that someone had bulldozed down to the waters of the Great Australian Bight. We couldn't resist it and took the heavily overloaded bikes down there. A shelf of rock at sea level had once contained petrified tree trunks, but these had been eroded away leaving vertical pipes through the rock. They now acted like fountains, and whenever a wave came in under the shelf it produced water jets of different heights. Going back up the road was a comedy. It consisted of broken limestone on a bed of sand, and it was steep. I took quite a bit of it on my rear wheel, with Charlie laughing himself silly at the faces I was making. Then we had a 200km ride before we could get a beer.

There were lots of bikes on the road and a lot of dead kangaroos next to it. People will insist on driving across here at night. The crows and enormous Wedgetail eagles were gorging themselves. A stop at Newman's Rocks, one of the few waterholes along the road, refreshed us and

The XL swings aboard the Kota Singapura *in Perth, on the way to Singapore. We had already covered over 3000 miles in Australia*

the long, sweeping bends as the road drops down from the plateau made riding interesting again.

We arrived in Norseman, the first town since Ceduna 1,000km to the east, in quite good spirits after spending three days out in the desert. The new tarred road really makes the crossing easy. Norseman boasts a good, traditional pub that serves passable pies as well as Swan Lager. Highway 1 took us down its narrow, potholed length back to Esperance, which is blessed with truly beautiful beaches of fine, white sand and clear water; it's also cursed with the most comprehensive collection of signs forbidding anything that might conceivably be fun. We spent the evening, thoroughly depressed, in one of the local dives called, would you believe, 'Casa Tavern'.

Before leaving Sydney, I had wangled an invitation to stay with the west coast correspondent of *Two Wheels*, the bike magazine I was writing for. I now rang this unfortunate to advise him of our imminent arrival and to ask him for some help with tyres and spares. I'd forgotten that it was Sunday morning, and got him out of bed. That wasn't to be the end of Ray's troubles with us. The rest of the day was spent dodging road trains—trucks with two and three trailers—and squeezing past a huge, wheeled hay rake someone had managed to arrange immovably across the highway. When we made camp, we could just see the outline of the Stirling Ranges through the evening haze. A short detour took us up to the foot of Bluff Knoll, where PAW, with an unerring eye for the most objectionable siting, had built an enormous brick toilet block so that you could see it 20km away. Bless their furry little heads. The Stirlings are still lovely, their steep but soft slopes covered in evergreen forest.

We lunched at Albany in the London Hotel, feeling rather homesick. Our local in Balmain is also called the London. It was a good lunch, too, and reasonable value for money. You can tell Western Australia is a prosperous state—food is dear and the people are dour. Wealth doesn't seem to cheer people up at all. We didn't put our tents up that night, but slept in a little hollow in the sandhills at William Bay, cosy on thick grass. We swam out to the rock bar across the bay, and there was a gorgeous sunset. After Walpole, we reached the forest of great karri and jarra trees which covers much of southern Western Australia. The café at Pemberton had an old Seeburg jukebox, stocked with records of the appropriate vintage, and we amused ourselves playing 'Running Bear' and the like. After a day of riding through chocolate-box scenery, we camped near Busselton and were confronted by a rather scary array of enormous insects. I've no idea what they were, but they were huge and looked nasty. None of them bit us, I will admit.

We found Ray's house when we got to Perth, and the key was in the letterbox as promised. By the time he got home from a hard day at the scrambles track we had emptied his refrigerator of Swan Lager. We sang the Swan Lager Song in an attempt to mollify him.

'Swan Lager, Swan Lager, you killed my old man,
Swan Lager, Swan Lager, kill me if you can, . . .'
The agents for Palanga Lines, with whom we were to sail to Singapore,

were helpful and told us to bring the bikes down to the wharf on the morning we were due to depart. Formalities were minimal. In Sydney we had been told to get here a week early, so we now had that week on our hands. The time passed quickly enough, bikini-watching on Perth beaches. We also located an old Singaporean pal of ours who was running his own restaurant and discussed Lee Kuan Yew, the Angels and the martial arts with him. Hoppy knows more than most about all three.

Ray and Kerry hosted a very small (the four of us) farewell party on the night before our departure. The number of empty beer cans this produced is now, I believe, a legend around the *Two Wheels* office. Badly hung over, we watched the bikes being slung aboard the *Kota Singapura* and then tied them down ourselves. They were down in the hold with a shipment of live sheep. Once boarding started, we staggered up the gangplank and found ourselves some deckchairs. Then we broke open the flagon of wine which we had, with uncanny foresight, rescued from the previous night's debauchery. Just as well, for the bar didn't open for hours. Cabins were quite comfortable, there were a lot of congenial people on board, and it didn't take long for the trip to take on the atmosphere of a cruise. I started a waterpolo competition, which was incredibly rough and lots of fun. To be able to tell the teams apart, we played beardies against cleanskins. Us beardies cleaned 'em up every time.

I also met Annie, the attractive, petite lady of whom you will be hearing more later in the story. A shipboard romance! You see, it does happen.

On talent night, we presented a musical version of Waltzing Matilda —for the cognoscenti, it was the Queensland version—a traditional Australian poem concerning a sheep thief. Australian legends are almost exclusively about thieves of one kind or another. Charlie rustled a real sheep from the mob in the hold. It's stage debut was rather spoilt by the

Charlie's bike is the centre of attention on the quay in Singapore. 250s are actually 'big' bikes in this city, where the normal bikes are 50s. The police ride Honda 450s

fact that it crapped all over the dance floor. Still, we were all nervous. . . .

The Paper Tiger—Singapore's preoccupation with paperwork— sprang as soon as we berthed. It was a Sunday, and therefore not possible to arrange the multitude of documents necessary to get the bikes off the ship. The ship was going back out into the Roads as soon as the passengers had been offloaded, and would not return until Wednesday. Palanga's agent was unhelpful to the point of being rude, and we had to settle for a bus ride to town.

Most of our fellow passengers were on a Sea-Jet tour to Britain, which included a hotel stopover in Singapore and then a cattle jet to London. The driver of the bus taking them—and us—to their hotel was an optimist and pulled the old 'whoops, we just happen to have stopped outside the shop of my brother, why don't you just look in' routine. I spotted a little Chinese hotel across the road and we ducked off the bus, leaving my camera case behind. After checking in at the Tong Ah, I discovered my loss quickly enough—and nearly had a heart attack—but the case had been offloaded at the tour hotel and I had no trouble getting it back.

Before Annie flew out to London, we had a couple of marvellous days together. We shopped, sightsaw and, of course, dined. Down by the harbour we discovered the statue of the 'Merlion', Singapore's heraldic beast. It bears a plaque reading 'The Merlion is a mythological beast created by the Singapore Tourist Board in 1975.' With Annie gone, it was time to tame the Paper Tiger, so we went down to the insurance office for Third Party insurance, valid in Singapore and Malaysia; to the Singapore AA for an import licence and a circulation permit; to the shipping office for a delivery order, and to the wharf for . . . the bikes? Oh, no! First the bikes had to be lifted out of the hold. They were covered in a stinking film from the sheep with whom they'd shared their home. Then the wharfage had to be calculated. A clerk measured them, over the extremities, and arrived at a figure of two cubic metres each. This was transmuted, by the magic of arithmetic, into a weight of two tonnes each. Just wait, I thought, until Soichiro Honda hears about his new 2-tonne trail bikes.

Clutching a form given to us by the measurer, we then had to queue for a delivery list. A very thorough questionnaire with three copies, this form actually demands the time of day—in two places. Is this some way of measuring how fast you fill out forms? Is there, perhaps, a prize? 'Most Improved this month goes to Charlie and The Bear, who have come up. . . .' A very kind Indian fellow-sufferer helped us wade through this.

We paid the wharfage and got the bikes, which refused to start. After a lot of pushing, swearing and checking of spark, we located the trouble. The carburettors were blocked by muck no doubt settled out of the petrol by the vibration on board. Red faced, we ran the gauntlet of Customs and police, who checked all the papers. The sergeant in charge, a large Sikh, had a brother in Sydney who was stationmaster at Coogee. There's no railway station at Coogee . . .! Singapore traffic, here we come.

Chapter 4

Conquering the Paper Tiger

South-East Asia

SINGAPORE TRAFFIC ISN'T nearly as bad as it looks at first. You just have to remember that the pedal-powered trishaws have the ultimate right of way and know it, that the trucks and buses that look as though they are about to carve you up *will* stop, and that it's all a bit of a joke on the part of the drivers, really. One of the few jokes about in Singapore.

We took full advantage of the city's attractions over the next few days: eating in Coleman Street; watching Chinese opera in Sungei Road; eating in Arab Street; delicious roti praha across the road from the Tong Ah for breakfast; drinking the superb fruit juices made from real fruit in front of your eyes. It's a bike city, but most of them are 50 and 70cc tiddlers. Suzuki were advertising their 'power alternative', an 80cc stepthrough. We saw a well-preserved Norton and two Gold Wings as well as a number of ex-War Department BSAs with girder forks and large sidecar boxes. Even some of the 50s had boxes on the side and delivered everything up to lengths of angle iron.

Singapore is a clean city. It might be more accurate to say that it's quite compulsively spotless, except for the waterways. Fines for littering are astronomical. I could well imagine living there for a while, but only for a while. It's all a bit too heavily regimented and conformist for comfort. When the time came for us to leave, we rode out on Changi Road and back around the reservoir to the border post at Woodlands. The border itself, out on the Causeway, was much easier than coming in. The gentleman processing us at the Malaysian border was in civvies, and we had a little argument. I maintained that a Carnet de Passage was necessary for Malaysia and he disagreed. 'Perhaps I'd better see a Customs officer,' said I. He drew himself up to his full four feet ten inches, threw me a withering glare and replied, 'I *am* a Customs officer!' What else could I do but accept his ruling? We rolled out into Johore Baharu and soon found the way to Tinggi. A good if slightly bumpy road took us up into the hills and the rubber and oil plantations. We stopped for a moment to don wet-weather gear and saw a chilling tableau. Up the hill, into a blind corner, came two trucks side by side having a drag on the narrow tar. I was very glad we weren't coming the other way....

In the little hotel in Tinggi I renewed my acquaintance with the dipper that takes the place of the shower in most South-East Asian countries. You just ladle water over yourself out of a large cement trough. Marvellously refreshing after a hot, sweaty day. A little farther up the coast we filled our tanks for the first time in Malaysia and discovered that a full tank costs about as much as a hotel room and three meals put together. This proportion was to hold true in most places.

We rode on up the east coast, jungle swamps alternating with hill plantations. I cashed a traveller's cheque at Mersing in a bank guarded by a little bloke armed with an enormous shotgun—bit dangerous being a bank robber here, you could get *hurt*. Lunch was consumed at the harbour, overlooking the colourful fishing fleet. All the boats had eyes painted on their bows to enable them to find their way through the shallows. People were only too happy to be photographed and I snapped some enormous grins.

The little village of Nenasi, where we had intended to stop for the night, didn't have a hotel, so we went on to the regional capital, Pekan. Dinner of excellent Kway Teow and fried and boiled noodles rounded off the day and we retired under the gently rotating ceiling fan. We left the luggage in the room next morning and rode the unburdened bikes up the beach. It was great fun and pleasant to be out of the traffic. The South China Sea looked so inviting in the heat that we stopped for a dip, but rather warm water made it less refreshing than it might have been. When we came out, our feet had suffered a sea change—not into something rich and fine, as Bill Shakespeare has it, but into something black and sticky. The beach was full of blobs of half-solidified oil. There was a fresh coconut lying on the ground near the bikes, and after a struggle I managed to get it open with my clasp knife. We found the milk refreshing and the meat delicious. By the time we rode back to town, the sun was high and very sharp. Fortunately we still had our shipboard tans and didn't burn. Despite my tan, I was feeling pale and fat alongside the slim, beautiful Malays.

The Sultan's museum provided quite a bit of amusement. All his possessions seemed to be kept there, from the stunning collection of Kris knives to his old toothbrushes. You could even admire his used underwear, lovingly labelled. We also found that Malaysian TV wasn't very Malaysian. After the news, they showed The Osmonds, and that was followed by Combat—dubbed. It was fascinating to see Vic Morrow opening his mouth and fluent—if badly synchronized—Malay coming out.

A bit of bad luck rather marred the next day. Just out of Kuantan, I glanced down at the map on my tank box. Charlie braked at exactly that moment for a large pothole and I ran into the back of his bike. Never look at maps on the move. . . . By the time we'd picked ourselves up, it was obvious we were in a bit of trouble. Charlie looked as though he'd just been subjected to the amorous attentions of a sandpaper python and my arm and shoulder hurt abominably. Charlie had lost a lot of skin and had a deep cut over his hip.

The hospital sewed Charlie up and put my arm in a sling despite my claims to a broken shoulder-blade. I dragged myself off to bed feeling like death warmed over and still sure I had a broken shoulder-blade. When you've broken as many bones as I have, you know the signs.

Charlie commandeered a truck from the nearest bike shop and went out to get our steeds. Everyone was marvellous from the chap who drove us to the hospital to the people who looked after the bikes. They were fixed cheaply and well while we convalesced. One night, we went to the local fleapit to see 'Romulus and Remus' with—guess who—Steve Reeves. The film was looking its age. Kuantan was a pleasant enough town, but it did become a little boring, and we filled in the time with eating and drinking—mostly steamed dumplings and fish, washed down with the local Guinness or Tiger beer. Then Charlie had his stitches out, and we were off again. Significant parts of his anatomy were still swathed in bandages and I couldn't lift my left arm. I had to use my right hand to put the left on the handlebars. We must have looked a fine sight rolling up to the first army checkpoint on the road to Raub. There had been an attack on a police station and the army obviously thought us likely suspects because they searched the bikes from stem to stern. But we were carrying neither explosives nor Communist Party membership cards so we were allowed to proceed. Once out of range of all the hardware being waved around, I started breathing again. I hate guns.

In Raub, we were invited to park our bikes in the kitchen of the hotel. Then we went out and had a magnificent Chinese dinner, peering out of the windows at the army and what I took to be militia, who were riding around on Yamaha 70s with fierce-looking shotguns slung over their shoulders. Charlie went out to the hospital in the morning to have his wounds dressed, and on the way out of town we were nearly run over by an armoured car.

There was an even more ingenious parking space for the bikes the next night: the hotel clerk's living-room. He had his own bike in there as well. Another visit to the movies rewarded us with 'The Buccaneer', a 1958 epic featuring Yul Brynner with hair. When we got back, the disco downstairs was going full blast. They were playing 'Rudolph the Red-nosed Reindeer' and 'Auld Land Syne'. Funny town, Kampar.

The road to Penang was a main highway, with ferocious traffic that ignored our poor little XLs completely. I kept expecting to have to choose between ramming an oncoming bus in the grille or ploughing into a gaggle of schoolkids on pushbikes. Tough luck, kiddies. . . .

Once off the ferry in Penang we checked into New China Hotel, of which I had pleasant memories. I even got my old room back. Then it was back to the hospital and another X-ray. I wasn't going to put up with the pain for much longer. 'No wonder you're in pain,' the doctor said. 'You have a crack as wide as my thumb in your left shoulder-blade. . . .' So I was grounded for a week, and Charlie chauffeured me about on the back of his bike. We filled in the time pleasantly with Magnolia ice-cream, coconut drinks and lashings of satay with peanut sauce. As well as getting our Thai visas, Charlie had a new rear wheel spacer made up for his bike. The old one had worn away to a slim circlet of metal. There were some other bikers staying at the hotel, including a German bloke on a Honda 500/4 and a Dutch chap called Frank, who had ridden a Harley WLA outfit to Nepal and stored it there while he and his lady looked at Malaysia. I amused myself scribbling puerile philosophy in my diary. It's amazing what your mind will turn to when you're not feeling on top of things.

What is it they say about all good things having to end? I loaded myself up with painkillers, gratis from the hospital, and we took to the road again. I must say, despite the slight mis-diagnosis at Kuantan, that the Malaysian hospital system is absolutely first class—and free, except for a nominal registration charge.

Charlie after his close encounter with Malaysian gravel. The bikes have already been repaired in this photo, but both of us still had a bit of healing to do

On our way up to the border we passed Butterworth Air Force Base, with only a slight pang of homesickness at the Australian flag flying over the gate. It's an Australian base, the only overseas one our forces have, and I guess it's designed to protect the Malaysians from . . . err. . . . The road to the border was enjoyable, with a good surface and long curves through hills covered with rubber plantations. It looked exactly the way it had ten years before when I came through on my bicycle.

There was comedy at the border. The Customs man wanted our Carnets. We told him about the bloke at the Singapore border and he started tearing his hair out. Of course we needed them! What did those clowns think they were doing? We left him still distraught and headed for the Thai border, several miles farther along the road. More comedy at Sadao as we fill out handfuls of forms that make the Singapore Paper Tiger seem like a tabby. This is the Paper Dragon. One form had eight carbons, all but the first two totally illegible. Each copy required a duty stamp, with the total charge being somewhere around 12 cents. Then several officials had to see, stamp and sign the forms. Most of these gentlemen were out to lunch, so we joined them. A tip for you—the coffee shop across the road from the Sadao border post gives an excellent exchange rate. Tell 'em The Bear sent you.

We managed to get away in the end and ride the few miles to Sonkghla, the first large town in Thailand. After finding a hotel we went out to the beach for drinks and dinner. We both sat in deckchairs out on the sand and then had a few more drinks. We were drinking Mekong, the well-known Thai whiskey, which allegedly gets its name from the river because it looks and tastes like it. Later, very much later, we tore ourselves away from the pretty little ladies who had been serving us—if truth be known, they closed up—and rode back to our hotel. Very slowly, very carefully, very crookedly and cursing the inadequate lighting on the XLs. Don't ever drink a lot of Mekong; it's not particularly strong, but the hangovers are awful.

The banks were closed the next day—it may have been Sunday—but we did manage to change some money at a large hotel and get out of town. Had Yai, which is the railhead for Songkhla, was dusty and confusing and we were glad to get back to the highway, but not for long. We were now open to attack from the huge Isuzu trucks that infest Thai roads, and spent quite a bit of time on the dirt escaping from them. Hangovers abating, we rode through country like a Chinese woodcut. A couple of local lads tried to teach us how to pronounce Phangnga. They were agog when we lit our pipes. The Governor of the province, it seemed, smoked a pipe, so no one else did—the neighbours might think they were getting above themselves. We had another beer in the Governor's honour and then the lights went out—just a power failure, not a sign of official disfavour. The next day we rode on to the 'Holiday Paradise' of Phuket Island, where we got directions for Patong Beach, the alleged hippy hangout, and rode out along an atrocious dirt track for a few miles. Right at the end was Patong Beach; we knew it was that because there was an enormous neon sign saying Patong Beach Hotel.

The place was inhabited by Germans on package tours, but we checked in at the rather more modest Palmgarten and invaded the bar pavilion to sample some more Mekong—some people never learn—and watch the first squalls of the monsoon bending the leaves of the palms. A few days of that convinced us that we'd better move on or be rained in, so we said goodbye to Sai Jai, the Thai lady in charge, and her assistants. Charlie had become rather, shall we say, friendly with one of these ladies and left her an esoteric Australian T-shirt. Both of us felt better for the rest and made an impressive 573km to Thap Sakae. On my bicycle tour, I had inadvertently spent a night in a brothel here, which had turned out to be a good hotel as well, but I couldn't find it again, so we settled for a lovely old timber hotel, all the wood lovingly oiled and spotless.

By the time we got to Bangkok, I had something else besides my shoulder to worry about—sunstroke. How do you get sunstroke while wearing a crash helmet? By exposing the base of your neck to the sun, that's how. I had been wearing only a singlet and the vicious sun had cooked my spinal fluid. It sounds worse than it was, actually; I just felt deathly ill for a few days and couldn't keep any food down. After I recovered, Charlie picked up a case of Bangkok belly. The city itself was slowly disintegrating. Roads and footpaths were crumbling, the klongs or canals were stinking cesspits and as for the power lines. . . . there was a bit of a thunderstorm when we arrived, and some of the powerlines had been blown together by the wind and were fusing, spitting sparks across the road and writhing in the air as they melted. Most street corners have their tangle of old, discarded wires aloft, ends waving in the breeze. Who knows which ones are live.

We booked into the Sri Hualampong Hotel and our bikes once more found a home in the lobby, the desk clerk lovingly spreading newspapers

A commercial vehicle in Kuantan. The loads these little step-throughs carry are amazing—and so is the bureaucracy. All the information painted on the back of the box is legally required

under them. While I was getting over the sunstroke, I lay in bed and listened to the frequent rainstorms drumming on the tin roof of the factory next door. I also drank gallons of the fresh tea that comes with the room. Once recovered, I sat downstairs in the lobby restaurant drinking beer and making occasional forays out into the city. Strange as it may sound, Bangkok is a stimulating, fascinating place even though it is falling apart—or perhaps because it is. . . . The only thing that really makes it possible to live in Bangkok is the fact that it's inhabited by Thais. No one else could possibly be so stubborn and relaxed in the insane traffic. No one else would be cool enough to survive. My hat off to the lot of them.

Not being Thais, we were quite glad to be taking the road out and heading north to Chieng Mai and within the first 30km we counted four buses that had dived into the rice paddies by the side of the road. After that, as we turned off to the ancient capital of Ayutthaya, traffic eased up a little. So did the rain. Ayutthaya is worth visiting for its more or less well-preserved temples and Buddhas, monuments to the lavish devoutness of Thailand's Buddhist rulers. But don't buy the soft drinks. Being located at a major tourist stop, the refreshment stand charges up to ten times the prices common elsewhere.

For some reason I developed a craving for a tomato sandwich on black bread during our ride on to Tak. Thai tomatoes are weedy, weevil-eaten woody midgets and Thai bread is dry, sweet and indescribably awful. So that was one impossible dream. . . . Our hotel in Tak was another of those marvellous all-timber buildings, the wood hand-polished and lacquered; probably a dreadful fire risk, but so lovely. We reached Chieng Mai the next day after dodging in and out of the clouds along the mountain road between Thoen and Li. Like most Thai roads this one was quite well surfaced and twisted enough to make for interesting riding. It was also lined with forests of dripping, ghostly mountain bamboo.

I'd love to know why they put direction signs so far past intersections here. Why not right at the crossroads? This way, you never know if you've taken the wrong turn until you're a hundred yards past the fork, where you have to turn around and try your chances on another track, and go through the same thing again.

Our base in Chieng Mai was the Chumpon Guest House, a spotless building with a commonroom, a garage and constantly available iced water. They did our washing for us, too. We found ourselves a tailor in town and ordered safari suits with long sleeves. (I have this theory that you get better treatment at borders when you dress up, so we were taking advantage of the cheap tailors.) A couple of days passed pleasantly with visits to the working elephants, the waterfalls and the endless 'antique' shops that dot the town. The night after we picked up our suits, we went on a spree. This mainly involved having dinner at the Chalet, a ritzy French restaurant. We felt we deserved it, and what's the good of new clothes if you can't show them off? Dinner was a huge success with pepper steak and steak Dijonaise set off beautifully by a '73 Medoc. It cost a fortune, but we felt like kings when we walked out. This sort of thing is highly recommended on any bike trip. Get out there and live every now and then, and a tent in the rain will be more acceptable for it.

I sent my mother a buffalo leather cut-out figure from a shadow puppet play. The Australian Customs opened it, I later discovered. I wonder what they thought I was sending my saintly old mum from Thailand?

On the way back down to Bangkok we visited another ancient capital, Sukothai—Thailand is lousy with ancient capitals—which was pretty, with the ruins all laid out in a grassy park that rather reminded me of Khajuraho in India. At the entrance, a policeman showed a rather unhealthy interest in the contents of my camera case. I fought off his increasingly stern demands to let him dig through it and was greatly relieved when we got away.

At this stage, apart from my sparkplug burning out and being replaced and a slight oil leak around the head gasket on Charlie's bike, we had had no problems. We rode on to Phitsanlok, a rather ordinary railway town made interesting by the total absence of tourists. Our white faces and beards attracted rather more than their usual interest as we wandered around after dark. The next morning I did what I had been dreading I'd do. I didn't take my passport and traveller's cheques out from under my pillow when we left, and didn't discover the fact until we'd been on the road an hour. Naturally we raced back as quickly as we could, and the desk clerk gravely handed the stuff back to me and refused a tip. I really don't deserve the nice people I meet.

We took a different route this time, up over the mountains, and had beautiful scenery for the rest of the day. A lot of forest, alternating with little corn fields so steep that the farmers use ropes to get their crops down.

Penang taxi in Pitt Street. Muscle-powered rickshaws are being replaced by motorcycles

Traffic was light on Highway 21 towards Saraburi, and the road good. We rode through a thunderstorm that felt just like riding through a river, it was so dense. The sun came out immediately afterwards and we were dry in half an hour. The sunset, over limestone cliffs, was dramatic. We made Saraburi well after dark, and for once the hotel had separate beds. This is unusual in South-East Asia—single rooms contain a double bed, double rooms contain two double beds. Hmmm.

The short ride to Bangkok was enlivened by all the tiny Villiers-engined three-wheeled delivery bikes on the road. They looked cute. We got back to Bangkok on Buddha's birthday and checked into the Sri again. Since we had been invited to park in the lobby last time, we just jumped the kerb and roared in. I'll never forget the faces of the people in the restaurant as the bikes suddenly burst into the quiet of the lobby like motorized samurai. Next day we repacked our belongings to take maximum advantage of the 20kg baggage allowance we had on the plane to Kathmandu, and took the bikes out to the airport early in the morning. Eight hours of frustration followed. First, we had to make pallets for the bikes; we were sent over the road for timber and nails, borrowed a hammer from Customs and set to. Then there was the problem of reducing the dimensions of the bikes as much as possible. Like the wharfage in Singapore, air freight charges went by the maximum dimensions. We took the front wheels off, lowered the bars, removed the panniers, let the tyres down and unscrewed the mirrors. Charlie did most of the work, being a more dab hand with the spanner than I, but I had work to do, too. I had to rush over to the main airport buildings to arrange the paperwork, a replay of Sadao, but urgent and without much help. An urchin found forms for me. To cap it all, we had to bribe a Customs officer to make sure the bikes got on the plane, the only time I have ever done that. We were dog tired and seething with fury—an interesting combination—when we got out to the road to catch a bus back to the Sri. Eight hours in well over century heat, without much shade and with constant frustrations.

Then the Great 21 Bus Mystery hit us. A gentleman at the bus stop told us we wanted a 21. So we climbed on the first one along, to be told that it didn't go past the Sri. 'You want a 21.' We were puzzled. 'Isn't this a 21?'—'Yes, but you want a *21*.' We were beginning to wonder if 'twenty-one' wasn't perhaps the Thai word for, say, 93. The fourth 21 finally took us. Back at the Sri, we immersed ourselves in beer and refused to come out. I sat there looking at a pepper pot with a winged bomb on it as a trademark and had some nasty fantasies involving Don Muang Airport.

Out at the airport the next morning to catch our flight, I realized that I'd packed my ticket in the pannier, which was on the bike, which, in turn, was already in the hold of the plane we were about to board. Full marks to Thai International. They listened to my story without even cracking a grin and issued a duplicate ticket.

The first scotch after take-off tasted like—well, like the first scotch after take-off. Nepal next, and Nepal was a nice place.

Chapter 5

So this is Shangri-La?

Nepal and India

The pontoon bridge at Ghazipur does far better service than a more permanent structure would. When the Ganges rises, the bridge rises as well—and doesn't get washed away

I ENJOY FLYING with Thai, not only for the free scotch and champagne but also for the friendly cabin crews. We had a relaxing trip and arrived at Tribhuvan Airport in Kathmandu in good shape, where I discovered that I had not only packed my ticket in the pannier but my passport photos as well. The pleasant immigration man waived the requirement of a photo for the visa and let me through. An amiable three-hour wrangle with Customs followed about the bikes. They finally accepted our Carnets and we were free to pick up the machines. 'Pick up' was right, too. Our carefully constructed pallets had disintegrated and the bikes were on their sides, Charlie's leaking acid from the battery. A friendly bystander brought us back a gallon of petrol from town and we wobbled off on near-empty tyres looking for a service station. We finally found air at a tyre shop. Service stations don't stock it.

Once in town, we parked in Freak Street and looked for accommodation where the bikes could be parked off the road. An Australian lady, a computer programmer turned trekking guide, recommended the Blue Angel. Being Marlene Dietrich fans, we checked in there. It was roomy and clean and had a carport where the bikes could be chained up.

Despite being one of the most unsanitary collections of buildings in the world, Kathmandu is a comfortable, relaxed town. It's fashionable to think that all places are spoilt in time, but Kathmandu seemed better to me in 1978 than in 1970, when I'd last been there: fewer out-and-out derelict hippies, apparently less hard drug usage and a less frenetic street life, but all the little chai bars and restaurants were still playing 'Dark Side of the Moon'. I introduced Charlie to the peculiar Nepalese idea of European cuisine. We ate things like mashed potatoes with mushroom sauce, buffalo steak, lemon pancakes like inner tubes and cast-iron fruit pies. Not as bad as it sounds, actually. Restaurants with names like Hungry Eye, New Glory, Krishna's and Chai 'n' Pie abound. The New Eden reminded me of an exchange I'd listened to in there a few years back:

American voice No. 1, in front of counter: 'Ah, how much are the cakes, man?'

American voice No. 2, behind counter: 'Chocolate two rupees, banana two rupees, hash one rupee.'

No. 1: 'Ah . . . how come the hash cakes are cheaper than banana cakes?'

No. 2: 'Because hash is cheaper than bananas.'

One morning we got up very early to go out to Nagarkot, a hill station near Kathmandu. We had hoped to get there before the mists rolled in and hid the Himalayas, but I got lost on the way, and all we saw was an enormous wall of cloud with Everest somewhere in the middle. Other daytrips went to Bodnath, the monkey temple; to the giant stupa at Swayambu; and to the river temples at Dashinkali. We also 'conquered' Pulchwoki, a 9050ft hill behind town, on the bikes, travelling on a 14km dirt road up to the top.

Wherever we went in the countryside, the roads were covered in freshly harvested grain sheaves. The locals thresh in the simplest way possible—by letting the traffic run over it.

There was a bike shop near the Blue Angel. I peered in one day and was invited to inspect the premises. The tools consisted of a screwdriver and a complete set of shifting spanners. Yes, well. . . .

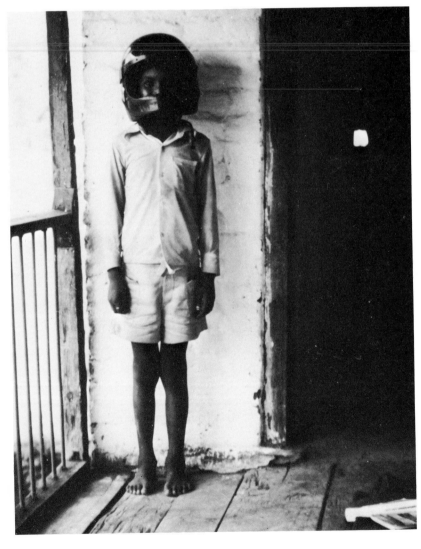

The youngest son of our host in Pokhara, Nepal, was fascinated by the bikes and anything connected with them. I gave him a lift around town and made his wildest dreams come true

We secured visa extensions and took off for Pokhara, Nepal's second city. The road was awful, more potholes than tar, until the turn-off to Birganj and thence India. After that it improved dramatically and was serviceable even despite the occasional mud slide or washaway. It was built by the Chinese and follows the shoulders of the river valleys over three low passes until it gets to the plateau that holds Pokhara. Charlie went off trekking, walking up in the mountains along the paths that serve the local people as roads. I checked in at a small, two-storey mud hotel and took it easy, bartering with the Tibetan pedlars, reading and writing. Tibetans are magnificent-looking people, like idealized Red Indians. They also have a great sense of humour. Being a little worried about drinking the water, I asked for a glass of boiled water at the hotel. I got it, too. A glass of boiling water—not quite what I'd intended, since I wanted to *drink* it. After that, I collected water from the roof during the frequent thunderstorms. The family running the hotel were very kind and kept offering me places in the buffalo stall for the bikes. I didn't think that was really safe; those buffs might be good-tempered enough but they were also enormous. The thought of one of them sitting on a bike was a bit worrying.

Pokhara itself is a long, narrow town as yet little touched by modernization. At one end it runs through large mango trees down to Lake Phewa, where the small hotels and shops catering for Europeans are. My shoulder was finally recovering, even though the torn muscles were still sore, and I just wandered around quietly. There was a lot to photograph, from the farmers arriving at the lakeshore in their dugout canoes to Machupuchare and the Annapurnas lifting their peaks high in the clear morning air. It's easier to see the mountains from Pokhara because the town is higher than Kathmandu, although you can't see Everest, which is too far away.

Charlie returned refreshed by his days in the mountains, and we took to the Siddhartha highway, heading down to India. Nepalese friends had warned us that the road was 'not very good': built by the Indian government, they shrugged. How right they were. The road is a nightmare of once-tarred dirt and gravel, but the scenery is superb—I think it was, anyway. As we came down through the deep river gorges, I wasn't often game enough to take my eyes off the road to admire it.

The Nepalese Customs man glanced at the souvenirs we'd bought and asked, 'Where's the hash?' with a grin and waved us through. We had donned our safari suits and the Indians were duly impressed; nobody asked for driving licences, insurance, vaccination cards or anything else except our passports—we were through in minutes. As we rode along shaded by great mango trees we diced with the traffic as far as Gorakhpur. Indian roads are alive with every kind of human, animal- and motor-powered transport imaginable. The truck drivers, being Sikhs, are pretty well unbluffable and all else moves too slowly to be worth bluffing.

The Standard Hotel provided a welcome cool room. A gentleman I took to be the owner insisted on buying us breakfast and involved us in a political discussion. It was his theory that Indians take politics so seriously because they can't afford any other kind of entertainment—politics are free.

We passed a funeral on the road that morning, the body wrapped in gold brocade from head to toe—a rather sad display of affluence among the drabness and obvious poverty.

In Ghazipur we had intended to change some money, and consequently went looking for the bank. Despite repeated sets of directions, we couldn't find it. Eventually someone took us right to the door. We'd been past it several times, but there was no indication that it was a bank. It looked like army barracks. It might just as well have been one, too; they would only accept US dollars. Not even sterling!

On into the increasingly hot day to Varanasi, where one of the banks had a 'late branch' in a hotel. We spotted a sign saying 'cold beer' just outside, and Charlie was despatched to investigate while I changed money. Not much luck for either of us. The bank clerk tried to give me rupees for $40 instead of the £40 I'd given him and turned quite nasty when I pointed out the slight discrepancy and Charlie discovered that the beer shop hadn't had an ice delivery for a couple of days and all the beer was warm. We retreated to the Hotel KMM, which had been recommended to us, and drank several gallons of tea and fresh lemon drink. It all went straight out again, through the pores. On an evening stroll through the crowds of holy men and pedlars we acquired a friend, an eight-year-old boy who wanted to sell us some silk. He tagged along down to the river and introduced us to his father, who had just had his evening dip in the holy river. We sat watching the sunset reflecting in the river as the father told us some stories about Varanasi and the Hindu gods. The next day was devoted to looking over such unique Varanasi attractions as the ghat on the riverbank, where corpses are burnt before being consigned to the sacred embrace of the river—a very quick look at that. Fighting off prospective guides took more time than anything else. We returned to our little friend's shop, in fact the family living-room and no doubt bedroom, and I bought some silk batik scarves for presents. They were beautiful, with motifs from Hindu mythology in rich colours.

It seemed to us that the best way to deal with the heat was to get up early, do most of our riding in the cool of the morning and rest in the afternoon, and with that in mind we rose at 4am to discover that there was a blackout. The electricity came back on at about the same time as the sun came up. We had loaded the bikes by the light of our torches. This little scheme worked quite well. It was still cool when we stopped in Mirzapur for a cup of tea at the railway station and the road outside showed us the reason for the blackout. There must have been a storm the previous night, because a number of poles had come down and filled the streets with a tangle of wires. We had a good road that day, still lined by mangos and quite spectacular where it climbed the edge of the Deccan. Our host for the night was a retired lawyer-turned-spiritualist who now ran a hotel in Satna. He assured us that, wherever we went in the universe, we would find people who spoke English. I guess a spiritualist ought to know.

A look at the erotic carvings on the temples at Khajuraho, which are incidentally very good and actually quite erotic, was followed by our hottest day to date. We pulled in to the courtyard of an Irrigation Department rest house and tried to find out from the chowkidar—the caretaker—if we could stay the night there and get something to eat. No luck. Our recently acquired few words of Hindi didn't seem to mean anything to him at all. Lady Luck chose that moment to arrive in the shape of a short chap driving a locally made Fiat with a hang glider on top. He told us later that it was the only one in the country and he had brought it in under the pretext that it was a tent—aircraft import duty would otherwise have been due on it. It appeared that we had not been able to communicate with the chowkidar because he only spoke the local dialect. Our new-found friend then reached into his car, where the thermometer read 52°C, and produced two bottles of beer *in ice* which he invited us to share with him on the verandah. I could have kissed him. The bungalow, he explained, was not set up for meals. We thanked him for the beer and rode on to Jhansi. The heat, all the worse now we knew just how hot it was, was coming up off the road like laser fire.

Jhansi's Central Hotel was pretty basic, with those dreadful short charpoys—beds made of timber and rope and designed for Indian not Australian bodies—but there was quite a good curry to be had downstairs and we were entertained by a wedding across the road. A lot of the wedding seemed to involve fire crackers.

Road works gave us a bit of trouble on the way to Agra. A row of stones across the road can mean one of two things—either there used to be a broken-down truck there that's been repaired and moved, or there's a bridge out around the next corner. It's not always easy to tell if the road ends dramatically a few yards farther on. We were also getting sore bums in the heat; XL seats are not comfortable. However, the Taj Mahal took our minds off our worries. It is the only building I have ever seen that lives up to the tourist hype, and we were fortunate enough to have a full moon to see it by. There were fireflies in the gardens, too, and it was almost unbearably romantic. Charlie and I would gladly have exchanged each other for a female companion.

We found lots of mail waiting for us in Delhi, but the money that should have been waiting at the bank hadn't arrived. In the lift of the bank, an Indian gent looked me up and down, said hello and ascertained that I was Australian and then asked: 'What is your purpose in life?' I was still trying to formulate a reply when we reached my floor and I beat a disorganized retreat.

The Tourist Camp looked rather more comfortable than most of the cheap hotels, so we pitched our flysheet there over a large bit of carpet donated by the manager. Charlie did a bit of maintenance work on the bikes, among other things replacing the rubber seal on one of the fork legs of my bike. It had been weeping oil and proved to be rather badly scored.

Visas were a headache. The Afghanis weren't issuing any, having just had a revolution. The Iraqis wanted our passports for three months, to send to Baghad for approval. At least the Iranians only took two days. Outside the Iranian Embassy we met Paul, a fellow biker from Chandigar who also intended to ride over to Europe. He invited us to come and stay with his family when we passed through Chandigar and we gratefully accepted.

We had a lot of trouble with our money transfers to Delhi and waited for over a week. It was partly the fault of our bank back in Australia, but the Indians certainly weren't overly organized. After we had covered Delhi's tourist attractions we whiled away the time in the US Information Service and British Council libraries. We also bought some sheepskins and made them into seat covers for the bikes. Our money came eventually; Charlie found the advice for his while glancing through one of the file folders in the bank.

Crossing the bridge out of town over the Yamuna River was like riding through a suburb of hell. It was a closed, boxy steel affair and hot, claustrophobic, slippery with dung, and it stank. The roads up to the foothills of the Himalayas weren't much, either. We passed a totally flattened three-wheeler van lying in the ditch.

We were on our way up to Rishikesh, yet another holy town. Hardwar, at the entrance of the valley, looked interesting with its hundreds of little shops lining the road, but Rishikesh itself was more like a Hindu Disneyland, complete with helicopter pads for the affluent gurus.

The road over to Simla was better. Lined by pine trees, it was chiselled into the sides of the hills. Every now and then the fog lifted and opened out spectacular views of hillsides and forest. There were some river fords, too, crossed amid much white water, and very little traffic, a great relief after the crush down on the plains. For a while the road ran parallel to the Simla railway, which looks like a big toy with its narrow gauge. Our stay with Paul's family was enjoyable too—they were Sikhs, very middle class and very kind. We had a little more maintenance to do—

Delhi fruit juices are superb. Made on the spot from fresh fruit, they can make all the difference on a muggy Delhi day. Charlie is pondering the relative attractions of mangos and pineapples

74

Charlie's bike was still showing a slight oil leak at the head gasket and my shift drum stopper bolt had shorn through. A friend of Paul's got his father to make us a new one, far better than the old, and Paul's brother JP arranged for me to go to the hospital and have a nasty boil on my arm lanced. When we left, the local boys had become rather dissatisfied with their bikes. The Yezdis they were riding, locally built Jawas, lagged rather noticeably behind the Hondas in sophistication. We left them trying to devise a way of improving the rear suspension to XL standards. The Grand Trunk Road swallowed us, on our way to Jammu and Kashmir. At a truck stop on the main road we finally managed to get a hot curry. Indians tend to be very solicitous of Europeans—they don't believe we can eat their curries. Charlie and I, being curry fiends, amazed this lot by going back for second helpings.

Just before Jammu we found a back road that would cut a few miles off the run to Kashmir, and followed it up into the hills. We also found that Charlie's engine was covered in oil ... he'd done the tappets in Chandigar and only finger-tightened some of the bolts. Then my clutch control started to slip. We still managed to enjoy the little back road, surrounded by fantastic cliffs carved out of the soft soil by rapid erosion. A bit dangerous, though. I can well imagine entire sections of roadway disappearing downhill in a rainstorm.

Staying at the Green Hotel in Udampur seemed like a good idea at first, until we discovered that there was no water and the room next to ours was being used for a party by a crowd of very drunk Sikhs from a nearby army base. Charlie refused to pay more than half of the bill in the morning and read the riot act to the proprietor in a way I still admire today.

The road to Kashmir is rather like a badly tarred motocross track, and about as much fun, which is to say that we enjoyed it as long as there were no trucks trying to run us off the road. Sometimes there was a drop of hundreds of metres (I kid you not) straight down from the edge of the road to the river, and no safety devices. Some of the mudslides across the road had been here so long they had been given names, on little concrete markers. I suppose it's easier than doing anything about them.... Just before we got to the 2·5km tunnel that leads to Kashmir we passed a military convoy of well over a hundred trucks. The tunnel itself is a nightmare with very poor orange lighting, no reflectors and icy drips from the ceiling.

Kashmir is a beautiful place and it's easy to see how it gave rise to the legend of Shangri-La, the paradise high in the Himalayas. Everything is green, there are majestic poplars lining the roads and the ground seems to ooze fertility. It has its problems, though, for the visitor. Kashmir is a holiday resort for thousands of people from India and is set up accordingly; the touts trying to sell you souvenirs, a hotel room, a bed on a houseboat or leather clothing can become *very* trying. They nearly threw themselves under the wheels of the bikes, business cards clutched in their hands, when they saw us coming. Ignoring them, we stayed in the faded Victorian splendour of Houseboat Golden Rod, our every wish catered for. Well, nearly. The Mughal gardens and floating palaces are worth seeing and shopping is good. We had some leather clothes made by Aruga The Robber (his shop sign) very cheaply, but alas not very well.

The road up is also the road down. We played chicken with another military convoy, buzzed through the heavily fortified town of Jammu—it's on the Pakistani border—and back out onto the plain. A South African bloke we met was travelling on a Dutch passport because South

The foothills of the Himalayas provide a magic world for the motorcyclist. The mists swirl apart and you can see the Ganges Plain, close in until it's just you, the road and the pines—and, very occasionally, they show you the great mountains themselves

Africans aren't allowed to enter India. He had a two-day-old Indian Enfield 350 with which he'd covered 200km. In that distance he had broken the throttle and front brake cables as well as losing the battery cover and the bolt holding the exhaust in place. He didn't think that was bad, and anyway there were bike repair shops everywhere.

We sent out for a couple of bottles of beer that night to go with our dinner, and when the waiter placed them on the table, one exploded. We made do with just one. There was an enormous crowd around when we loaded the bikes up in the morning. In a country of crowds, where you seem to draw them like honey does bees, you get used to them. This one was extraordinary though—commerce ceased as everyone watched us. We had to deliberately tread on people's toes to get to the bikes. It was scary, even though there wasn't the slightest feeling of hostility. A little later, the skies opened and the monsoon proper had begun. Within a few minutes the carriageway was 15 to 20cm deep in water—muddy water. This meant that not only was the rain obscuring our sight but the potholes were invisible too.

In the Amritsar Youth Hostel we met Jajime, a Japanese chap who'd ridden a Yamaha DT125 from Calcutta to Kayseri in Turkey and was now on his way back. He thought the DT was perhaps a little slow for the long roads. While in Amritsar we duly admired the Golden Temple, spiritual home of the Sikhs, and then headed for the Pakistani border. On the way, I swerved to miss an elderly gent on a bicycle and fell over. My chain came off and the inevitable crowd gathered while we replaced it. Charlie finally lost his temper and hit a young bloke who obstinately kept getting in his way. Not very hard, but I was concerned how the crowd would take it. They fell about laughing.

We crossed the border at the same time as an unbelievably well-equipped party of British mountaineers. They were Royal Engineers returning after a few months in the Himalayas on full pay. Could it be that there's something to be said for the army after all? Indian Customs and immigration processed us politely, though not promptly—they weren't together enough for *that*—while they bossed a motley crowd of hippies around rather brusquely. The Border Safari Suit Ploy works again!

Chapter 6

Where Islam rules

A village shopping centre on the way up to Kashmir. It may not look like much, but you can buy practically anything you want here—even bike parts!

This is the local bus that plies the Khyber Pass. It must have been a very quiet day—some of the passengers have actually left their rifles at home

Pakistan to Turkey

THERE WAS A dire shortage of pens at the Pakistani border post. All the guys kept borrowing each other's, which tended to slow things down a bit. I finally donated one of my treasured Nikkos to the bloke who was processing us and we were through in seconds. Bribery can be cheap.

On the dusty road to Lahore we noticed the difference in road manners compared to India. Everybody was much more together and aggressive, which made the traffic rather more predictable. The Australian AA guide book gave us a bum steer to the location of the Pakistan AA guest house. They didn't even have the right street. As a result it took us hours to find it, and we were sorry when we did. It wasn't so much the decaying cars outside or yet the mould on the walls and the broken windows, it was the constant drip of every tap in the place that bothered me. We took it anyway, because it was also dirt cheap. Then we set off to find some food and cheer ourselves up. The Capri Grill in the Mall provided excellent chicken livers and terrible chips. The Mall itself was well worth a look, with the enormous Zam Zam gun from Kipling's *Kim* at one end and the slums discreetly tucked away at the other. But even so Lahore is quite a leafy and attractive place; its Red Mosque is allegedly the largest in the world. You can go and look at it, too, which makes a change from all the closed houses of worship some religions go in for, which seems self-defeating to me.

The road to Rawalpindi looked like a left-over set from a disaster movie. It was difficult to decide whether it was being repaired or had simply been abandoned. We weren't clear of the monsoon yet, either, so we rode in a downpour most of the day. My speedo cable broke, too, but at least the weather was warm.

All the cheap hotels in Pindi were mysteriously full, and we wondered for a while if we had a disease that they could see and we couldn't. A kind gentleman explained that the government doesn't allow them to rent rooms to Europeans; Whiteys have to go to the dear ones. We moved into the Alia, which was comfortable and had room for the bikes in the lobby as well as an *en-suite* bathroom and toilet. This turned out to be just as well. . . . At dinner across the road, while trying to choose between the usual gristly mutton, athletic chicken and slimy marrow curries, we drank some water out of the bottle provided. Mistake. Our reward was a painful case of stomach bug. Both of us featured delicate pale green faces, dizziness, diarrhoea and a total inability to keep any-

Crash helmets were a never-ending source of interest. These Afghani truck drivers look solid enough to not need them

On the road up to Bamiyan, in the Afghani mountains, I took a corner too wide and found myself face to face with a minibus. That's why Charlie is fiddling with the bike; it didn't take to sliding on gravel. The shepherds were intrigued

thing in our stomachs for three days. Hence the use for the *en-suite* conveniences.

Somehow amongst all that we still managed to get out to the Afghani Embassy in Islamabad to apply for visas, where, they explained, the visa section was at Nigeria House, across the town. Who said there's no co-operation among Third World nations? Over to Nigeria House and, yes, we could get visas, for seven days. Come back tomorrow to collect them. It beats me why you always have to wait for visas, when all they are is a stamp in your passport. It's just attempted intimidation, I'm sure. We picked up the visas when we had recovered a little and headed for the border. Within the first couple of miles, we were both stung by monster wasps, the side of my face swelling up until I looked like a Dick Tracy character. The road north was pretty dull, but enlivened by the marvellously colourful trucks and buses; the paintings on some of them would be the envy of any California customiser.

Peshawar, especially the military cantonment, was pretty and green. At the gate to the Khyber road, there's a sign that warns you that once past the gate you're on your own—the government takes no responsibility for you. During the hours of darkness nobody is allowed in at all. It's not terribly hard to see why they're so careful. All the male locals carry bandoliers and well-used ·303 rifles, and they look *tough*. These are the Pathans of song and story, and they'd make it to President in any bike gang I've ever seen without even riding a bike.

The road through the pass is surprisingly good, although infested by cars and pick-up trucks all carrying more passengers than you'd think possible. They take the boot lids off the cars and passengers sit there and on the roof-rack while the family of the driver travels inside. Everybody grins and waves, which takes the edge off the universal toughness a bit. Villages feature high walls and watch towers. The border town is called Tor Khan and consists of a number of mud huts collectively defying gravity. One of the more ragged-looking edifices is the Tourist Hotel, which, while it may not have running water, does have cold beer as well as a very entertaining proprietor.

There are only two categories of the compulsory Afghani vehicle insurance—vehicles with more than eight seats or fewer. This meant that we had to pay the same rate as a minibus. But we got our own back on the Customs bloke. He only knew three words of English, 'I must look ...', and he kept saying them as he stood in front of our carefully packed and locked machines. We said 'OK, look,' and ignored the fact that he wanted us to unlock everything. He finally took readings from our odometers to cover his embarrassment and left, muttering 'I must look....' If you don't understand our glee at beating the Customs for once, you've never been through a bad border. Our joy didn't last long, of course. Within a few minutes, still in the pass, I had a flat tyre, our first on the trip. There was a largish tack in the front tyre, which we fixed as quickly as possible, because it was hot again and there was no shade. We were well and truly out of the monsoon now, and would see no more rain until the Black Sea.

Jallalabad was a friendly if slightly rough town, and we stopped for one of the local hamburgers and 20 bottles of coke. The old bloke deep-frying the meat asked us if we wanted salad. Is the Pope Catholic? Of course we wanted salad. He gave us each a great handful of chopped onion. Then on to the middle of town where there was an intersection featuring a lot of those fiddly little cement islands, meant to channel traffic in the right directions. We were still getting used to riding on the right—it changes at the border—and wove our way around in different but about equally wrong paths. The policeman on point duty watched with an open mouth.

We swam in the icy Kabul River just below Kabul Gorge, one of the most spectacular bits of roadbuilding around. The road just climbs up a vertical rock wall, with switchbacks and tunnels every few yards. At the top of the gorge an XL went past us, going the other way. Huh? Paul, the rider, was on his way home to Australia from Britain. He had made the mistake of riding at night in Iran. A broken arm had taught him not to do it again.

At a roadblock near Kabul, the army checked our papers. The officer in charge looked at our passports and said, 'Aha, Australia. So you do not speak English?' We solemnly shook our heads and he waved us through. Next came our introduction to the game of buying petrol. To understand how this works, you must know that the pumps only show quantity, not price. So you fill up and give the attendant some money. He stands there and smiles at you. You hold out your hand and demand change. He gives a little start—oh, sorry!—and gives you a little money. Then he stands there and smiles at you again. You repeat your act, he repeats his. This goes on until you either have all your change or give up in disgust. It's best to have the right money in the first place.

The Desert of Death in northern Afghanistan is aptly named. We had a flat tyre here, and fixed it in temperatures well over 130° F. We also drank over a gallon of water each while we did it

There was no trouble finding a hotel, and then out for dinner on Chicken Street, a thoroughfare full of shops selling genuine antiques. 'But of course these bracelets are genuine antiques! Did I not make them myself only yesterday?' We ate delicious minced-meat kebabs and drank delicious tea in one of the many filthy, comfortable chai khanas, or tea houses, and took stock. Our visas weren't long enough for us to take a trip up to Bamian, but we both wanted to see it. One-week visa extensions took four days to get, which wasn't really worth it, so we decided to simply overstay and pay the fine when we left.

A day was spent in the dusty and totally enchanting Kabul bazaar, watching absolutely medieval things like the water delivery—it comes in goatskins. Then it was off along the Mazar road, a well-surfaced tar highway to the Russian border. After about 100km, we turned off onto the 160km gravel track to Bamian. The track winds through the Koh-e-Baba mountains, with some breathtaking gorges and blasted, lonely plateaux on the way. I was a bit too keen and encountered a minibus as I was taking a corner on the wrong side of the road. Result, one dropped bike with twisted forks. We straightened them by the roadside, watched by a trio of goatherds, and not long afterwards I had another flat tyre. But, let me add, none of this spoilt the ride for us.

A young teacher invited us in for a cup of tea and we discussed politics. He was in favour of the Communist revolution which had just taken place—the first of three which culminated in the Russian takeover two years later—but he was violently anti-Russian. I wonder what he's doing now. . . .

Bamian, which is nearly three thousand metres high, was cool and quiet. We moved in at the Marco Polo Motel—the owner insisted that the man himself had stayed there—and went off to inspect the magnificent

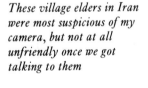

These village elders in Iran were most suspicious of my camera, but not at all unfriendly once we got talking to them

Iranian drivers are very, very strange. One moment they're trying to run you off the road and the next they're offering you tea and melons. Charlie ponders the contradictions

A Turkish trail bike

50m statue of Buddha. This was carved out of the rock in the fourth century, when the monastery here had thousands of monks. Genghis Khan chopped its face off some 800 years later. Genghis also destroyed the old city of Bamian, now an eerie collection of ruins on a hilltop called the City of Noise. The Ajar Valley, around the new Bamian, is an oasis of fertility in the grim mountains, kept green by irrigation water brought many kilometres from the melting snows. Tourism has done its work, unfortunately; the children greet strangers with 'Hello, paise'. Paise is the local word for—money. We looked at the Red City on the way back. This is another ruined town, built of red mud and now melting down the cliffs in the infrequent rains. Then, on the road again, I did something very foolish. Thinking I had been seen, I made to overtake a truck on the right. Just as I was level with it, the driver pulled over and ran me off the road. I went down a nine-metre embankment, weaving my way through the boulders, into a field, where I stopped the bike and shook for a while.

Back in Kabul, we couldn't believe ourselves in the mirror. We were covered in a fine, grey dust and looked about 90 years old. A shower soon fixed that, however, but at a price. The Kabul water supply also comes straight off the melting snows, and you step out of the shower blue with cold. Still, as everyone says, it's very refreshing. The next day, after admiring a number of well-preserved police BMWs with sidecars, we had cholera booster injections and departed.

Filling up in the Khyber Pass

The Kandahar road is dull, but the surface is good. We had intended to stop in Ghazni, but the government hotel had no water and the alternatives were dirty and expensive, so we pushed on to Kelat. Along the way we saw an Afghan Hound herding some sheep, the only time I've ever seen one of these beasts at work. Further on a small boy thought he'd impress his friends by throwing a rock at me. Now I don't think this sort of thing is a good idea at all, so I turned around to go back and point out the error of his ways. He took off across the fields, running for all he was worth, and lost his cap, his satchel and the respect of his friends all at the same time. After a night in the hotel-cum-police station at Kelat (we couldn't work out which it was) we made Kandahar without further incident, except for the Attack of the Suicide Sheep, that is. For some reason best known to themselves, a mob of these stupid animals tried to throw themselves under our wheels.

A break in the appropriately named Peace Hotel in Kandahar and we were ready for the 1000km Dasht-i-Dargo, the Desert of Death. We stopped for a swim in the Farrah River, the only body of water between Kandahar and Herat. When we took the bikes down the river bank, a

With the sun high in the sky standing without head protection can be dangerous. Even a heavy, hot crash helmet can be safer in the Desert of Death

thorn lodged in Charlie's back tyre and caused a flat when we were back in the mountains. We drank something like five litres of water each in the time it took to fix the first and then the second flat, which we caused when we disturbed an old patch. It was *hot*. I can see why they call it the Desert of Death.

The electricity in Herat was a bit … *thin*, I suppose. An American chap we met had been using a 120-volt shaver in the allegedly 240-volt sockets without trouble. Our patience ran a bit thin, too, as we rushed around from one government office to the next trying to pay our fine for overstaying and getting exit permission. The border was easy in comparison. We had been warned of people hiding drugs on our bikes and then reporting us, so we stopped short of the border and searched the bikes ourselves. Nothing. At the Afghani border post they didn't even search us. The Iranians were a little keener. They seemed set to give us the sort of thorough going over a Land Rover was getting in the next parking bay. But then, when they brought out their bit of bent wire to probe the insides of our petrol tanks, I pointed out that they didn't need it. The plastic tanks were translucent. That impressed them so much they let us go on the spot. We left them prising the lining out of the Land-Rover.

We made it to the Mashad campsite and sat down to calm our nerves with a beer, our first encounter with Iranian drivers behind us. Iranians are the worst drivers in the world. They think nothing of pulling out to overtake a bus that's passing a truck that's passing another bus—on a blind corner. They are also unfamiliar with the use of the gears. On flat roads, they drive in top gear with the accelerator flat to the boards and they don't change down for hills. As a result they were passing us on the flat and we were passing them on the hills. This brought out the homicidal maniac in them, since it is apparently a deadly insult to pass a car on a bike. They would chase us and run us off the road. Consequently, we spent a great deal of time in the dirt, getting up the nerve to go back onto the tar. Every police station has a stone plinth outside with a particularly badly mangled car on it, presumably as a warning. Nobody takes any notice.

Very carefully we rode up to the Caspian Sea and then back down over a stunning pass to Tehran. At night we camped with all the locals in the parks every town has on its outskirts for this purpose. The people who had been trying to kill us all day couldn't have been nicer; they helped us to find water, offered us tea and melons and gave us cigarettes. Then, the next morning, they went back to trying to kill us.

Tehran traffic is so bad that we didn't even try to cope with it—we took the minibus to town from our campsite, the famous Gol-el Sahra. Charlie managed to find some XL spares, including a new speedometer cable for mine. We also did some maintenance work. Then we decided to skip our planned excursion down to Esfahan—to be perfectly honest, I just refused to go—and headed straight for the border.

Our last camp in Iran was at Maku, behind the Maku Inn. It sticks in my mind because I managed to find some proper bread, thick and moist, a great treat after the dry stuff Iranians eat. Once again people were most helpful and very friendly. I have nothing against the people in Iran—as long as they're not behind the wheel of a car. At Maku we also met a couple of Swiss guys on XT500s fitted with 31-litre tanks. They were going to tackle the middle road through Afghanistan, which not only has no petrol stations but no road either.

At the border, we buzzed past the enormous queue of TIR semi-trailers waiting to be processed and got through quickly and easily. Then we had to wait. There's a two-hour time change at the border and on the Turkish side it was before business hours. While we were waiting we chatted to the people going the other way, who were mostly Germans going to jobs in Iran. They gave us helpful advice as well as a couple of gallons of petrol and a map of Turkey. There are so many nice people out there. Once the border opened, we asked about insurance and were told that, yes, we had to have it. But the nearest place it was available was Erzurum, 200km to the west. Mmm. We rode off without it, and nobody cared.

At Dogubayazit—the locals call it Ozit, with rare good sense—we turned off the Asian Highway and headed up towards Kars. Although this road was slightly longer, it avoided the pass and the dirt road at Agri. The road wasn't bad at all despite a lot of gravel stretches and we spent the night at the rather nasty Pasinler Inn. Charlie was feeling unwell and went off to bed, and I had a major battle with the desk trying to change

Mount Ararat sits by itself at the eastern edge of the Anatolian highlands. The Turks, like the shepherd in the foreground, are keen cigarette-cadgers. Sometimes, when they don't get any, they get mad enough to start throwing rocks

a traveller's cheque. Once they realized they wouldn't get paid if they didn't cash it, it was no problem.

Erzurum looked grim, and we didn't bother stopping for insurance.

It was exhausting getting to Trabzon on the Black Sea. The road was a fine example of the Turkish 'too hard' syndrome. Wherever it ran over flat country it was in good repair; as soon as it approached one of the three passes and went up into the mountains it deteriorated alarmingly. My theory is that it's easy to fix flat roads, but mountains are too hard. Lunch was at a little lokanta in the hills, and a truck driver who had worked in Germany for a while, like so many of his countrymen, warned us about the locals. 'The Turks can't drive, they're crazy.' They're not as bad as Iranians.

When we came over the last pass, we headed straight down into cloud and rain. It stayed with us until we left the Black Sea again. At the campsite in Trabzon we met an Australian couple in a Range-Rover who had just spent three weeks camped at a petrol station waiting for a delivery so they could fill their tank and go on. We carried every ounce of spare petrol we could from then on. Scenery along the coast was pleasant enough but hardly stunning, and the constant drizzle dampened our spirits. Charlie, intrepid soul that he is, had a swim in the Black Sea. We then struck the touring rider's bane—roadworks. There was mud on the road, and passing trucks threw up a fine film that settled on my spectacles and turned them opaque. Once out of that, we had a dice with a John Deere combine harvester; for once, we won. Back on the main cross-Turkey road, the traffic became a problem and I nearly killed myself when I misjudged the speed of a truck I was trying to pass.

Ankara was dreary and dirty, but the campsite was a welcome little oasis. The guard looked like Rochester from the Jack Benny Show and refused to let us camp on the grass—we had to put up our shelter on the rocky verge. He also claimed to speak six languages, but they all turned out to be Turkish.

Our next destination was Cappadocia and the rock houses of Göreme, so we turned south. We rode past the salt Lake Tuz on good and dreadfully straight roads down to Nevshehir and Göreme—there was a little trouble getting petrol but not much and we made it through without delays. 'Paris Camping' supplied hot showers on our first night, but then we moved down to the Rock House Hotel. Some enterprising local souls had laid down a few carpets in one of the old stone houses and had turned it into a hotel. It was not exactly luxury class—the bathroom consisted of a puddle half-way up the hill and the toilets were the surrounding vineyards—but it was cheap and interesting. We pottered around for a couple of days looking at the truly amazing carving—what could be more amazing than a carved *house*—and then continued south towards the coast. Just out of Nigde, the spring clip holding the rear wheel spacer on Charlie's bike gave out. In one of the neatest pieces of open-road surgery I have ever seen, he fabricated a new clip by hacksawing a piece out of the spare spacer from Penang and bending it together. A good man to have along is Charlie.

We buzzed down through the ferocious traffic in the Cilician Gates, the main pass leading to the Middle East, and had a lunch of half-raw roast chicken in Mersin. Yuk! We regretted our decision to spend the night in the grandoise BP Mocamp at Silifke, too—the allegedly hot showers were cold and the staff must have been specially selected for insolence. And it was expensive! Things improved after that, with the road becoming more interesting as the coast became more rugged. It's pretty country, and campsites jump out at you from under the pine trees—unofficial campsites. We spent one night high up in the hills sitting around a fire and feeling thoroughly at peace with the world.

At Göreme, the soft rock of the famous 'rock houses' is slowly melting away. The roadway is supported by meticulously laid stone walls

A photo spanning two continents. Charlie, in the foreground, is still in Asia— but the houses visible in the background are already in European Istanbul. The Bosphorus lies below

A quick look at the famous Crusader castle at Anamur and a dip in the Med prepared us for another day on the road, although it didn't prepare us for the couple we met driving a camper van with an 'Australia' sticker on the back. I'd gone to school with Alex, and Charlie went to University with Carol's brother. Do you want to say it or shall I? Small world, ain't it. . . . .

In Antalya they were tarring both sides of the main road and the detour through the lanes wasn't signposted. We saw every back street in that town at least twice before we got out. Then we came across a chilling sight—row upon row of little asbestos-sheet huts on the beach, behind barbed wire. We thought it was a concentration camp, but it turned out to be a holiday village.

The Kemer road was pretty again, with pine forests and cliffs and a little café under the trees by a waterfall. But our nemesis, roadworks, struck again and we struggled through bulldozed mudbaths to Kas. This picturesque little fishing village lies at the foot of a 300m cliff, is very attractive but lacks a campground, so exploring along the dirt track that pretends to be a main road west of here we found a sheltered beach where we could camp.

Charlie's bike was beginning to worry us now. It was difficult to start and had begun to leak oil badly around the head gasket. Doing the timing didn't improve things and it became obvious that two of the head bolts had stripped the thread in the barrel. After a glass of tea at dozy Kalkhan we tackled the gravel section we'd heard of. It was interesting, all right. I took it at speed and got so far ahead that Charlie turned around to see if he hadn't passed me without realizing it. After we got together again, my bike went into a terrifying tankslapper at about 80km/h. I'll say this, I didn't fall off. No thanks to my riding ability; I just hung on, and I think I screamed. Then Charlie was very nearly skittled by a tractor that turned across the road in front of him. But the people were nice to us, gave us vegetables and let us camp on their land.

A short but scary run with the traffic on the main road, the E23, took us to Istanbul and over the great new toll bridge to Europe. At the Youth Hostel near the Blue Mosque our bikes once again found a home in the lobby. Istanbul traffic looks quite terrifying, but isn't all that bad on a bike. We met a couple of sad-looking blokes at the post office who had been waiting for the third member of their party for two days. On the way out of town, he and his 650 Yamaha had disappeared. These two were leaning on their BMW and Honda 500 twin hoping he'd turn up. As they were headed for Australia they still had quite a way to go.

We went for a ferry trip on the Bosphorus, ate hugely at a little snack bar specializing in shish kebabs, shopped at the Grand Bazaar and finally left for the Greek border. Then the bike misbehaved, spluttering and refusing to pull. For those of you who can no longer stand the suspense, it was the timing. It was checked later with a strobe and found to be way out. So don't try to do static timing on an XL, OK?

The border was boring. But then, very few borders aren't, and I'd rather have a boring one anyway. Excitement at borders generally means trouble.

Chapter 7

'Play Ramona again, Sam'

Greece to Ireland

Not far now! The good ship Avalon *took us from Fishguard to Rosslare. On arrival, we were sprayed with disinfectant....*

IN GREECE, LIKE Turkey, they write your bike into your passport so you can't sell it and disrupt the economy. If, on your way out, you can't produce the bike, they don't let you leave. With this in mind, and knowing that Charlie would be flying out to a genetics congress in Moscow, we asked Customs to write both bikes into my passport. As I would be looking after them until Charlie came back, that seemed reasonable. Not to Customs it didn't. First they were very suspicious of this trip to Moscow, which Charlie had unfortunately mentioned. Was he going off to get instructions from the Kremlin? Then they decided it was against the law to bring in more than one bike on one passport. Then the bank at the border wouldn't sell us any petrol coupons. Bikes didn't entitle us to them.

Our first impressions of Greece were sorted out over a lunch of calamari and retsina in Alexandropoulis, and we weren't sure we liked it. After the third bottle of retsina we mellowed, and that night in Kavala we decided it wasn't such a bad place. We spent the evening sitting at a sidewalk café, listening to a trio with two clarinetty things and a bass drum playing something that *didn't* sound like 'Zorba', and had a few beers.

We couldn't quite work out what was happening in Thessaloniki. There were tents everywhere, in parks, squares, even in parking lots. A Boy Scout convention? No, it turned out that there had been an earthquake and nobody was game to go back into their houses. Around this area bike cops abounded, mounted on machines as varied as Nortons, Moto Guzzis, BMWs and, of course, old Harley Davidson Glides. The local bikers seemed to favour the 50cc Kreidler Florett.

Time was running out—Charlie's congress started the next week—so we found ourselves a campsite down on the Halkidiki peninsula and settled in. I wrote to Annie, who was then supposed to be in Athens. Charlie went through all the Customs hassles that we had hoped to avoid, putting his bike into bond so that they would cross it out of his passport. The bond turned out to be an underground car-park. He even had to pay the parking fee when he came back! Once alone, I settled into a happy routine involving eating, sleeping and visits to the taverna, with a bit of swimming thrown in. Annie arrived, looking edible in her Chicago Bears T-shirt, and we spent an idyllic week together. She had to go back and start her Eurail pass then, and Charlie returned. He brought his tent, which an obliging fellow scientist had brought all the way from Australia. He also had a box of genuine Havana cigars and a bottle of Russian vodka, with which we celebrated his return in style. New tyres went onto the bikes and we moved to Thessaloniki to get something done about the stripped threads in Charlie's cylinder. He had spotted a shop advertising helicoiling. The mechanic took a look at the bike and nodded, sure, he could helicoil that. Then he retapped it to a larger bolt size. What happened to the helicoiling, we asked. Helicoiling? Oh, *heli*coiling. They didn't do that, any more. We went and had another beer. The bolts worked fine.

Yugoslavia looked great at first. Even the autoput, famous for its state of disrepair, was in pretty good nick. We hid away in a bit of forest, since free camping is not allowed in this country, and set up the tent. The rain started early in the morning, and it became obvious to me as we rode up into the dripping hillside forest before Prizren that my wet weather gear was due for retirement. Just after Pec, the alleged main road turned into a gravel path, then a goat track and then it started crawling up and down an endless procession of ridges. It got colder, it got wetter, and I became more and more miserable. Charlie was at least dry! The bikes handled the 'road' quite well, but I'd hate to do that stretch on anything but a trailbike. I'd hate to do it again on a trailbike!

A tiny pub saved us, high up on a ridgetop. It provided brandy and hot bean soup, and it was warm. The scenery was chocolate-box pretty, and not much later the road improved as well. The last few miles to Titograd weren't bad at all and we saw lots of other bikes, mainly touring BMWs with German plates. The Titograd campground had the loveliest lady at reception and hot showers. We camped under the damp trees and, feeling human after the shower, went over to the restaurant for some dinner. Since there was a 'music charge' if you ate in the main restaurant, we settled for sitting with the help in the kitchen and listened to the strains of 'Ramona' and 'Charmaine' filtering through the door for free.

The Kotor hill with its hairpins, rotten surface and steep drop impressed us greatly, as did the tour buses using it at breakneck speed. There was another cloudburst just after we left Kotor Bay and we arrived sodden in Dubrovnik. There was even water in our panniers, a most unusual occurrence. We splurged on a *pension* to dry out. The *pension* made a good base for exploring the old walled city. We wandered around the steep stone paths, admired the medieval buildings and splurged once more, this time on a top-notch meal. Despite the heavy emphasis on tourism, Dubrovnik seemed a pleasant place to us. A pity that most of the tourists were so dull and conservatively dressed. The few Americans made a pleasant splash of colour with bright T-shirts and Bermuda shorts.

We had clear sky and sun most of the way up the coast. The hills are quite stark here, dry and infertile and the ranges look as though they've been hit with a gigantic mallet and shattered. Jagged rocks are every-where, and we had a little trouble finding a place to put the tent.

94

Coming up to the Italian border, the temporary circlip Charlie had made in Turkey broke again. He had to use one of the spacers fitted to the bike to make another, which led to a great deal of play in the rear wheel. We jumped the two-mile queue at the border—motorbikes are invaluable for that—and got as far as Trieste. No, signore, XLs are not imported into Italy. So there were no spares. What now? The bike was pretty well unrideable in its present state, and eventually the rear wheel would of course fall off. Charlie, being an incurable optimist, decided we should make some spacers out of a spare inner tube. Being a decidedly curable optimist, I pointed out that Soichiro Honda would hardly make spacers out of steel if rubber would do. Unfortunately I was right. The bike ate the rubber spacers on the autostrada. We got the can opener out and made some more out of the tops of oil cans. Did you know that they use really thin metal for oil cans? We made dozens and hobbled along periodically making more until the hopelessness of that solution finally sank in. We camped in a laybay near Vicenza and slept with our heads inches from the traffic roaring past. A bike shop came to our rescue in the morning; they turned a new, thick spacer and fitted a new circlip, and we had no more trouble. I was so grateful that I bought a set of rainproof overalls from them.

Cheered by all this success, we decided to get an idea of the real Italy by taking the back roads. After a number of suicide attempts under our wheels we returned to the autostrada at Verona. Italy was a bit too hectic. Tolls aren't expensive for bikes on the autostrada and we buzzed along in fine style, passing Milan's enormous suburbs and turning up to the Alps. We forgot to use our last petrol coupons at the last station in Italy. Anyone have a use for a 10-litre Italian petrol coupon?

There was a little hut at the border selling Green Card insurance, so we finally weakened and bought some. Of course, no one asked for it when we crossed. Camp that night was right on the lake at Lugano, comfortable and quiet, and a pleasant change from the previous night.

I made one of my famous mistakes the next morning. We had a choice between the St Bernhard tunnel and the St Gotthard pass, and I thought: Who wants to spend such a lovely day underground? So up into the Alps we went, past the trucks cleaning the roadside gravel (it's true! They do) until it started to drizzle. With wet-weather gear on, we continued. The drizzle turned to snow, and we were still nowhere near the top. Instead of turning around we pressed on and finally made the pass in the driving snow. We were not exactly dressed for snow, and had even disposed of our visors some time before because they had become too scratched to be safe. Ice formed on our beards and my glasses. I have never been so cold in my life. On top of all this, the Swiss have a charming habit of cutting parallel grooves in the road surface. No doubt this is useful in preventing cars from sliding all over the place in snow, but it imparts weave to small bikes. A welcome pub supplied coffee and brandy once we were below the snow line, and we continued to Zurich in the driving rain. What the hell, it was only rain. . . .

The border with Germany was complicated. Our road first crossed

95

to Germany, then back to Switzerland and then back to Germany again, all in the space of about 16km. It was lucky that we had bought Green Cards in Italy, because this time everybody wanted to see them. The Germans also pored over all the exotic stamps in our passports for a while and I thought they might decide to search us. But no, they'd just been curious.

It was the middle of September by now, and Germany was quite cold. We slept in our clothes that night and the next, but then, after a long day on the autobahn, we arrived in Brunswick and my aunt and uncle made us welcome. They fed us up for a few days and my aunt dropped our clothes into the washing machine. We couldn't believe that it was actually possible to get the stuff clean again. We visited more relatives in Luneburg and Hamburg and then rode over to Amersfoort in Holland to stay with Frank, the Harley rider we'd met in Penang. A marvellous evening followed, recounting woes and laughing about mishaps. All very easy to do afterwards.

After crossing Belgium in something like an hour, we turned down towards Paris. The autoroute is quite expensive, and you can't get a glass of wine in the restaurants—in France of all places! Our friends in Paris, Campbell of BMW R60 fame, and Mimin, were away for the weekend. We camped in the Bois and had a look at the famous city. When they returned we moved over to their flat and spent a few days being deluged with French hospitality. Campbell wanted to go over to London to buy

Arrived at last at the fount of all wisdom—Charlie explains our trip to the astonished gatekeeper at the Guinness brewery in Dublin

RIGHT *The Dublin mountains, where I cut my motorcycling and touring teeth, have been a constant lure to me ever since. This is some of the finest riding country in the world and I re-visit it almost annually on a succession of different touring machines. This is the much-travelled Yamaha XS750 at Lough Tay near Glendalough on Christmas Day 1978*

BELOW *The Desert of Death in northern Afghanistan. We fixed a flat tyre here, in temperatures well over 130°F, and drank more than a gallon of water each in the process!*

LEFT *Kashmir shopkeepers can be disarmingly honest in their advertising! Aruga made us some leathers quite cheaply but not very well*

RIGHT *The Atlas mountains are spectacular, the local roads slightly less so . . . Does Evel Knieval like touring?*

BELOW RIGHT *The Magic Roundabout dubbed in Portuguese was an added attraction at the Sines campsite en route to the Algarve*

BELOW *The Suzuki outfit proved a bit of a handful in the narrow streets of the Algarve towns in southern Portugal*

The road through the Atlas to Ourzazate is one of the highlights of any North African tour

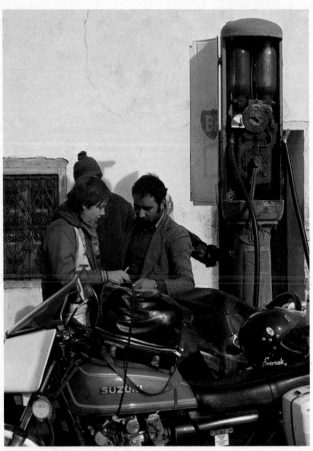

LEFT *Annie pays the fuel bill at a typical petrol station in the Atlas mountains*

BELOW *If you want to get away from it all, try the Sahara! The flat expanse of nothingness grows dull very quickly; we decided to turn back in search of more exciting terrain*

Houseplant gone mad! The XL250 and saguaro cactus make an excellent study in still life

a bike, so when the time came we offered him a lift. The bikes looked like overloaded camels as we transferred some of my load to Charlie and Campbell crouched behind me. We still made good time to Boulogne, through the rain, but then the hovercraft didn't want us. No bikes allowed on Seaspeed. We took the normal ferry and actually had a dry road from Dover to London.

I bought some new wet-weather gear and we took off again, into a headwind to Wales and the lovely hills above Swansea. Then Charlie's throttle cable broke. We had a spare, so it didn't matter, did it? The spare turned out to be a return cable, which is not interchangeable with the actuating one. Only Honda design engineers know why. Kevin and Skippy, a young Welsh couple, came to our assistance. Skippy got her name from the fact that she'd spent some time in Australia as a child. They showed me a bike shop where I secured a new cable and then invited us over to their place. We spent the evening in the weirdest pub I have ever seen, the walls covered in comic book characters, and enjoyed ourselves.

Welsh roads were as much fun as Welsh people, and our enjoyment of the ride was only spoiled by mysterious headaches the next morning. The crossing from Fishguard was uneventful, except that they sprayed us with disinfectant when we rolled ashore in Rosslare. With both bikes running noticeably rough now, we spent a few days exploring the south of Ireland, especially enjoying the Ring of Kerry and a priceless bed-and-breakfast place in Portroe. On to Dublin and a hero's welcome at the Guinness Brewery, where they poured untold quantities of the precious fluid down our throats, stood us a truly magnificent lunch and had us interviewed for radio and papers. Laden with gifts, we retired to our room and tried to come to terms with the fact that the trip, for now, was over.

Chapter 8

Chasing the sun for winter

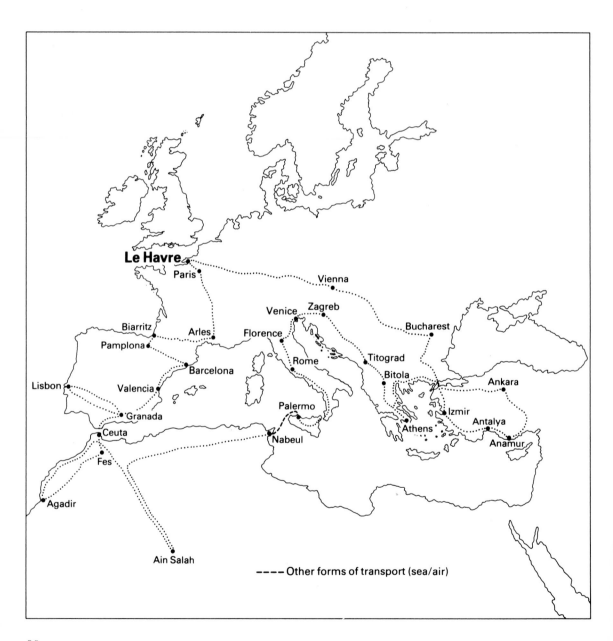

Britain to Spain

ANNIE AND I had now enjoyed one winter in Britain, and didn't really want to face another. So the plans were made—we would go to North Africa for the cold months. Yamaha Germany very kindly offered us an XS1100 on loan, and we snapped it up. It was taken down to Vetter Industries and fitted with a Windjammer fairing as well as panniers and a top box. Neil and Millie, another Australian couple, decided to join us on their Suzuki GS750. This was fitted with a sports sidecar by Squire and the roomy luggage from Craven; Boyers also fitted their electronic ignition. None of us had camping gear for more than the odd long weekend, so we spent a morning with the folk at Binleys Camping Supplies in Kettering and staggered out fully equipped.

On 3 November, badly overloaded and not really fully prepared, we rolled aboard the ferry to France. It was dark when we reached Le Havre, but we had little trouble finding the campground. Not that it did us much good for, just four days earlier, the site had closed for the season. We set up camp in the park across the road, dined on sandwiches we'd made from the remaining contents of our refrigerator before leaving London, and slept very well. I always sleep better when it's free. . . .

The road signs and our maps were rather confusing in the morning, so although we had intended to follow the byroads to Paris we ended up on the autoroute. It was Sunday and the road was full of pretty bikes, all sharp and clean, and we felt rather out of place lumbering along on our overloaded camels. The Bois campsite extended its usual welcome, with deep mud and inoperative showers. It's not bad, actually. There are a lot of trees and it's quite close to the centre of the city. I do wish they'd fix those showers. About half of them just swallow your token, burp and give you nothing in return. Most of the others give you your few minutes of hot water, but there's always one that's stuck 'on' and therefore free. The procedure, therefore, is never to go into an unoccupied cubicle. Wait until somebody comes out of one and ask 'C'est marche?' before committing your token. If one shower has a queue in front of it, that's the free one. Wait for that.

If all the above sounds like too much trouble, imagine the frustration of getting undressed, putting your token in the slot without being rewarded with hot water, getting dressed, plodding over to the office to complain and get another token, getting undressed, putting your token. . . . The showers have been like that for 11 years now.

It rained during the night, and the top of the Lowrider tent Neil and Millie were using filled up with water, but surprisingly little seeped through. Neil and I spent the next day working on the bikes, finishing all the little things we should have done back in London. Some people from a minibus camped next door wandered over and gave us the wonderful news that they'd just come back from Morocco and it had rained all the time. After dinner, I found reassurance in a sip of my duty-free Glenfiddich and we once again donned our Damart gear to go to bed. It was cold enough to penetrate our down sleeping bags. A few days in Paris were fun, but the rain refused to let up and we pushed on towards the Mediterranean.

One of the alterations we had made to the GS was fitting it with GS1000 air shocks. As we rolled out of Paris, these proved to be underinflated, and as we could not work out how to get more air into them without losing oil, we changed back to the old units. A wet day followed, with occasional glimpses of the lovely French autumn countryside as we rolled through the forests. We had a picnic at lunchtime—in an old disused petrol station at Sens. It was the only place we could get in out of the rain. After dark, I switched the XS onto high beam coming out of a tunnel and promptly blew a fuse. A few hectic seconds followed—there was a corner somewhere out there—before I'd stopped safely on the gravel. The original 10-amp fuse was obviously not enough to cope with the extra load of all the lights the Vetter gear features, so I replaced it with a $12\frac{1}{2}$ amp one and had no further trouble.

What a ride! In the three days it took us to make our way down to the Med, we discovered just about all of the defects our equipment was to show during the entire trip. The Vetter panniers leaked a little, and tightening the locks only cured one. To be fair, Vetter told us later that our panniers had come from the only less than perfect batch they'd had. The sidecar hood wasn't entirely waterproof either, and the occupant complained that it was a little claustrophobic. The GS battery refused to hold a charge and the XS happily followed every white line that presented itself. At one point I had to make a crash stop on the outfit, and the overloaded sidecar pulled me into the opposing lane, fortunately without dire results. At least the fairings proved their value; the Windjammer was excellent and even the little Corsair on the GS helped a lot in the rain. Tempers wore a bit thin, too. Luckily we found good campsites all the way.

It was a great relief to find some sun—not much, but some—in Marseilles. We camped at La Ciotat after a run along the coast road, where we had another chance to admire the local bikes. Mostly kitted out as endurance racers, they all seemed to be piloted by riders bent on suicide. They were fun to watch. Our spirits were restored by an excellent if horrendously expensive bouillabaisse, which was consumed with great gusto. We spent a few evenings in the 'Civette du Port', a friendly little bar where we fascinated the waiters by playing Scrabble late into the night. Our campsite wasn't very pleasant, and it was still so cold that we slept in our thermalwear every night. A short run to St Tropez wasn't terribly impressive, either. The coast road is plastered with 'Private Property' signs, forbidding picnics, camping and even stopping!

Renewed sunshine cheered us up again and we set off west along the coast in fine spirits. But France really didn't seem to be for us. Just past Marseilles, the GS suddenly developed a very flat tyre. Inspection showed four broken spokes, one of which had punctured the tube. The overloading was taking its toll. Neil and I respoked the wheel as well as we could beside the road, patched the tube and limped to the nearest campsite at Carry Le Rouet.

As if that last mishap had been the parting shot from our evil luck, things began to look up immediately. The campsite was comfortable and had excellent hot showers; a bikeshop in Marseilles respoked the wheel for us in a couple of hours; and the mistral started to blow the rain clouds out to sea. I did get lost on the way back from the bike shop, admittedly, and saw most of southern France before I got back onto the proper autoroute.... A major sortout followed and we sent three large, heavy parcels back home. My typewriter went, too—sadly missed; I hate writing longhand. Then we loaded most of the remaining heavy gear aboard the XS which hardly seemed to feel the difference. We were all breathing more easily as we buzzed off along the coast, over the classy motorway bridge at Martigues and on to Arles for an excellent lunch.

It is difficult to imagine how such flat countryside can be so beautiful, but the Camargue, with its waterways, stands of golden reeds and herds of white horses, looked lovely. With the mistral at our backs, we drifted through the meadows and occasional stands of umbrella pine down to Les Stes Maries with its little chapel that attracts thousands of Gypsy pilgrims every year. The town centre still felt quite medieval with its winding alleys and little shops, but a huge modern holiday development

Most campsites in Eastern Europe, like this one in Romania, offer little Noddy-houses as well as camping space. We stuck with the tent

all around rather spoils it. In the sandy campsite we did a little maintenance work on the bikes and I couldn't understand why it was impossible
to get the rear brake disc of the XS back between the calipers after I had
replaced the pads. Lots of headscratching later, it occurred to me that
I'd refilled the brake fluid reservoir as well. Sure enough, I'd put in too
much fluid. The spokes on the GS seemed to be holding. We tapped
them every day now.

There was still aggravation in our little party as personalities clashed,
and Annie and I took the opportunity to spend a couple of evenings by
ourselves in a comfortable bar by the harbour, drinking kir and gazing
into the fire. The bar mascot, a dachshund, kept us company. He had a
very simple way of indicating that the fire was getting too low—he would
crawl right up into the brick fireplace.

We moved camp after some days of this rather heavily touristed
environment; our new home was 'La Refuge', a tiny place in the town of
Vias. On the way, Neil once more puzzled the locals by asking where the
war was when he meant the railway station. His rather good French
always seemed to fail him when he had to differentiate between 'gare'
and 'guerre'. We also met a German lady on a Honda 400/4, who calmly
informed us that she was going down to The Gambia to sell her bike.
Carrying very little gear, she had been freezing in her leathers for the
last three days. We gave her some lunch and wished her luck.

Vias proved to be exactly what we needed—it was just a small wine
and tourist village in the off season. With friendly people and the 'Café de
France', where we became such good customers that the patron started
buying us drinks, the place was cosy. We had a couple of barbeques on
the beach and generally took it easy. Our bail bonds for Spain didn't
start for another eight days. I also had new tyres, Metzelers, fitted to the
XS at the Honda shop in Beziers. The rear wheel nearly reduced their
mechanics to tears, and it took them three times as long as they'd quoted
to replace the tyre. They swore they would never touch another XS1100.
I still don't know why—I've replaced a rear tyre on that bike myself and
it gave me no trouble.

Feeling more relaxed, we continued to Biarritz via Toulouse. A sunny
morning and pleasant lunch at Carcassonne were followed by a freezing,
impenetrable fog just outside Toulouse. With our heated handlebar
grips, electric GloGloves and Motomod Alaskan suits we weren't exactly
cold—but we still couldn't see. A campsite loomed out of the fog just in
time.

Our flysheets were frozen stiff the next morning and the fog was still
just as dense as the night before. We crept through Toulouse. An hour
later, the fog lifted and we had the sunniest day of the trip so far. Our
run that day through the hills of Gascony was nothing short of idyllic.
This was the home of cassoulet, Armagnac and foie gras, substantial
chalets peering out of the little copses and the snowy slopes of the
Pyrenees blinking away on the horizon. I kept seeing signs all day
advertising 'Chiens Bergers Allemandes' and my mind kept twisting the
translation to German Dogburgers, possibly competition for the

American fast food chains. They were only selling German Shepherds, of course.

In a little village just before our camp at St Sever, we passed a small church called Notre Dame du Rugby. Now that's taking sports to heart. St Sever is on the edge of the Gironde and lies peacefully in a wooded valley. Our petrol stove was acting up, giving only a low flame when it would burn at all. We consoled ourselves with a few drinks in the bar/tobacconist/newsagents/shop in the village. Even this out-of-the-way place had an electronic amusement machine, featuring little clowns breaking balloons. I was interested to see that the last 'human' score had been twenty, while the clowns by themselves often racked up 30–35. Clever little electronic clowns. . . .

It was cold again that night, but not unpleasant, and the next day we were nearly at Biarritz when the back wheel of the GS collapsed once more. Oh dear. We located the Suzuki shop in Bayonne, but they couldn't help until the next day. When we pointed out that this meant our sleeping by the side of the road, they gave us the name of another shop in Biarritz. After much pleading, the chap there agreed to rebuild the wheel for us, but he didn't think there were any heavier spokes available. We had to face facts. There was little point in laying out more money when the spokes would only break again. We had to buy a cast wheel. After an elaborate series of phone calls, our friend in the bike shop arranged for the other shop to stay open for us and to accept traveller's cheques. Neil raced back to Bayonne, bought the wheel, raced back to Biarritz, had it fitted with our wheel bearings, tyre and tube; and we put the wheel back on the bike. By now it was nearly 10 pm, and we had a great deal of trouble finding an open campground. Tempers flared. When we did find a site, we agreed that we must talk our frictions out.

Annie and I spent a relaxing day in Biarritz, where we picked up mail and had a picnic out on the beachfront rocks. Then we all got together for our bit of group therapy in one of the local bars. It emerged that Annie and I didn't really think that Millie could cope with this kind of travelling, and that she found me too bossy and overbearing. We thought she complained and niggled too much; she thought we didn't listen to her enough. We adjourned after a bit of healthy self-criticism, and things did improve quite noticeably for a while.

We crossed into Spain with minimal formalities and followed an awful, pockmarked road to San Sebastian. We stuck it out for long enough to buy a gas stove with a little bottle and then took to the hills. While the road didn't improve, the air at least became transparent again. The pollution was grim. We rode through some lovely autumn hill country to Pamplona, which was all rather spoilt by the amount of waste hanging from riverside trees. There were fun and games in Pamplona, with our blue Australian passports acting like the proverbial red rag to a bull. Every time we showed them at any of the *pensions*, they were suddenly and mysteriously full. It was later explained to us that Australians had a bad name for their behaviour during the running of the bulls. The boys must really have misbehaved to upset the Spaniards that badly!

We had to find somewhere to stay, because the campsites were all closed for the season and it was getting late. Finally someone relented, but Neil and I had to share one room and the girls another. It appears there's this law. . . . The bikes stayed out in the street, chained to a lamp post and to each other, with their alarms on. We went to do the bars and had a great evening. There was no need to go to a restaurant—the bars served delicious snacks such as liver with onions, pork and pimentos and grilled sardines, all of which we washed down with glasses of the cheap vino tinto. Wherever we went in town, we were greeted with cries of 'Inglese moto!'

The bikes were still there the next morning. An old gentleman told us that we had been 'loco' to leave them there, but couldn't offer an alternative. They weren't entirely untouched—someone had carefully peeled most of the stickers off them. Breakfast was by the side of the road as we had a long way to go that day. It consisted of jam on fresh bread bought from a van and coffee heated on our new gas stove. A great improvement over the petrol stove—it took less than half as long.

It was a long grind for the rest of the day, 12 hours down to the coast at Vinaroz, near Barcelona. The Ebro valley is flat and agricultural, and there was a great deal of mist, which hid anything that might have been worth seeing. Just before the coast, up in some hills and in the dark, we passed Morello and were spooked by the chill bulk of the castle hulking

Spain is a restorer's paradise. Imagine getting your hands on one of these Hispaniola Guzzis and returning it to concours condition

over the town. Had there been a lighted tower window, I could well have imagined a latter-day vampire sitting down to ... er ... breakfast.

Castel Camping offered another castle, albeit a fake one built out of concrete blocks, and iron-hard ground. The hard ground turned out to be a common feature in Spain. Take heavy-duty pegs if you go. The grounds were deserted when we arrived, but the owners, a German couple, returned from a night at the movies just as we were setting up. They were friendly, turned on the hot water for us, and we all went to bed—very tired. A little maintenance work the next day was interrupted by the arrival of a German tour bus. Its occupants spent the day in the site restaurant, listening to salesmen who were demonstrating kitchen gadgets. I couldn't contain my curiosity, and during their lunchbreak I asked what was going on. It appeared that they got a free bus from Germany in exchange for sitting down and listening to the sales pitch. Funny way to spend your holidays.

The coast south to Valencia was dreary and dirty. Every layby seems to be used as a rubbish dump, the rivers are open sewers and it's dull country. Valencia does have a good market and that, combined with the ridiculously cheap booze, reconciled me to the place. Our campsite was south of the city and surrounded by blocks of 'holiday flats'. We had a little potato bake on the beach and consumed a few litres of Sangria, but we felt as though we were being watched by the brooding concrete giants all around us.

Dreadful hangovers in the morning made packing a bit of a chore. Then, back on the road, both Neil and I kept imagining there was something wrong with the bikes—just Sangria withdrawal symptoms. But we certainly didn't imagine the bottle that burst on the pavement near us when we stopped to cash a cheque. I guess someone in the apartment block behind us didn't like bikes; they certainly had a very graphic way of showing it. We moved. The Costa del Fish 'n' Chips rolled past, looking grimmer than a suburb of Calcutta, and we camped in an excruciatingly expensive site near Alicante. Spanish campsites do not offer off-season rates like the French ones, and they're out to squeeze every peseta they can out of you. Nasty places.

It did become interesting, and more pleasant, after we had crossed the Sierra Nevada to Granada. A cosy campsite made up for the fact that we'd arrived on the Feast of the Immaculate Conception and everything was closed. The Alhambra was worth looking at, although it can hardly compete with some of the great buildings in the same style in India or Pakistan. The Red Fort at Delhi, for instance, is both more intricate and grandiose. Granada boasts good pastry shops, which we explored at leisure. Annie had what we assumed was an allergy reaction and her hands became itchy and covered in a rash. Antihistamine cream and tablets helped, but she had a great deal of difficulty sleeping. I think it had something to do with the amount of chlorine in the water.

On the way to Seville we passed quite a number of bike cops in pairs on their pitiful Sanglas 500s. A couple of them found it difficult to disguise their envy of the Yamaha when we pulled up, but tried to act

105

In one our least successful adaptations, we tried to fit Suzuki GS1000G shock absorbers to the GS750. Couldn't get them to work, though....

nonchalantly. Coming into Seville was a little like coming home. There are large stands of gum trees and casuarinas, both natives of Australia, but while the orange trees that line the streets look fine from a distance, the polluted air has done its work and close up the fruit is grey, the leaves crippled. There was the most glorious cathedral, though, with buttress upon buttress reaching out from the nave until it all looked like a cross between an enormous centipede and an equally huge spider.

The Portuguese border was next, through mountain ranges hung with mist and covered in cork oaks. The road was awful, like most Spanish roads, but offered pretty surroundings for a change. The undergrowth was inhabited by troops of pigs snuffling around for fallen acorns. Portuguese Customs checked our papers quite thoroughly, but gave us no trouble. The road just over the border was even worse than the Spanish ones, and for a while I held an image in my mind of us limping into Lisbon with totally ruined shock absorbers. But lo! Within a mile or so the surface became quite reasonable and stayed that way through most of the country.

We spent that night in the municipal campsite at Beja, a green and cheerful place that cost us a tenth of what the last site in Spain had. Things were looking up. I took us on a tour of rural Portugal the next day, when I confused the road signs, but no one minded. The road went through forests with the occasional village squatting in its fields.

Our first major town held a surprise. This was Setubal, which has the most diabolical one-way system known to man. It is necessary to traverse just about every street in town before emerging at the other side. I hit a pothole, too, that I thought was going to swallow the bike whole.

From the south, Lisbon is approached by a long, high suspension bridge. Neil, who was riding the XS, noticed that the bridge had no guard rail, and the gusty wind kept blowing him over to the side, and he didn't enjoy that at all.

You'd never have any trouble finding the campsite in Lisbon. It's so well signposted that you'd think the city was an adjunct to the site rather than the other way around. A pleasure to not have to search for ages. Lisbon itself is a homely sort of place, with good shops and pleasant bars. In the bars you can buy plates of seafood, including whole crabs. We toured the old town, the Alfama, on the outfit and had trouble fitting through some of the narrow, steep streets. There are excellent, cheap restaurants here, specializing once again in seafoods, and we had marinated fried tuna and grilled sardines. The people gave us good-natured advice—don't park there, traffic comes around the corner so fast! There was so much gesticulating that I understood Portuguese quite easily. Trams run through the alleyways, and on blind corners there are men with table tennis bats—one side red, the other green. When a tram comes along, they show you the red side of the bat and you stop. Portuguese policemen are rather more fortunate than the Spaniards and get BMWs on which to ride around.

It was Millie's birthday, and we bought her a cake, which was much appreciated. We also found a laundromat and did some long-overdue washing, and I invested in a litre of the cheap and delicious local pear brandy.

Going south again, we took the coast road through Simbales. It must have been a sleepy fishing village not too long ago, but has been caught up in the tourist trade now. A castle overlooks the town, looking suspiciously like a dozen other castles we'd seen in this country—I have a theory that they're mass-produced in cardboard and erected anywhere there are tourists, for atmosphere. Over lunch we were serenaded by a great flock of goats with bells around their necks. Shortly afterwards, I pulled out to overtake a truck and suddenly found a car coming the other way. I opened the throttle of the XS a little too far and we went past the truck on the back wheel. A rather unexpected bonus, considering the load we were carrying. . . .

Our map showed a bridge across the river mouth here, but that turned out to be a misprint and we had to brave the Setubal one-way system again. Then we did something very naughty—an oil change by the side of the road, running the waste oil into a pit and covering it up. Considering that everyone else does the same thing, without covering it up, we didn't feel *too* guilty.

In the Sines campsite we watched the Magic Roundabout on TV, dubbed into Portuguese; it didn't seem to lose anything in the translation, and Zebedee was as cute as ever. A German engineer we met suggested we take the mountain road rather than the coastal highway down to the Algarve. We were glad we'd followed his advice when we found a well-surfaced, twisting road lined with enormous gum trees and pine forests. We did have one heart-stopper along here, however. I had just paid at a service station when I turned around and saw the Yamaha wreathed in smoke. By the time I was half-way to the sidecar for the fire extinguisher, I realized that it was just steam, the attendant having washed some spilt petrol off the tank and the water had vaporized off the hot engine. Quite a relief.

We had organized the catering so that one couple bought the food and cooked for a week and then handed over to the others. When Neil and Millie handed over to us down on the coast, they had overspent badly and we had another argument. The goodwill of Biarritz was wearing thin. Then Millie was cheated of £14 changing money at the border and didn't notice until we'd crossed to Spain on the rickety old ferry. It wore even thinner. Regrettably, things that don't really seem to matter very much in normal life can take on great importance in the hothouse conditions of a long tour.

Our map showed a motorway from the border to Seville, but this turned out to exist only on paper, so we took longer to cover this stretch than anticipated. By the time we got onto the motorway to Cadiz, we were riding into the setting sun; and the last stage down to Algeciras was done in the dark. But it was a remarkably good road; we stopped for a roadside dinner with coffee and arrived at the campsite in good shape. Neil and Millie took the XS to Granada to pick up the mail and Annie and I did some shopping for Africa, mostly packet soups and a bit of booze. We also chatted to a chopper-riding Swede in the campsite who had just returned from Morocco. He made it sound just like every other Muslim country I'd been to.

We were at the wharf quite early the next day to catch the ferry, and Annie went off to mail some letters while we were waiting. Neil and Millie decided to get the outfit on board to make sure it was out of harm's way, and disappeared down the dock. Then, ten minutes before time, our ferry cast off and sailed! Annie returned and we stood watching our companions disappearing around the mole. Or so we thought. Just then, an elderly French chap I'd been talking with earlier came over and asked us if we weren't going to Ceuta. Of course we were, but—regardez, la bateau marche. Oh, no, he said. The Ceuta boat was farther down the wharf, but we'd better get there *toute suite* or it would go without us. ... Annie and I were on the bike, down the other end of the wharf and aboard the *Virgin of Africa* in a time that would have made Graeme Crosby proud. I always did have a habit of jumping to conclusions.

Chapter 9

Here's the Sahara but where's the scenery?

Morocco to Tunisia

The first snow in 15 years greeted us in the lovely Meknes campsite. Some people have all the luck . . .

GOING FROM SPAIN to Ceuta is just like crossing the English Channel; even the ferries are similar—the main differences are that you get a view of the Rock of Gibraltar and the crossing only takes $1\frac{1}{2}$ hours. Ceuta is rather like a dusty, grubby Singapore with all the atmosphere of excitement that freeports get. The mailing slot in the post office is the mouth of an enormous brass lion's head, which impressed me no end.

The border was slow, but fairly relaxed. We were apprehensive, having heard horror stories, but the only horrible thing that happened was that we had to lay out a fortune for insurance. Customs seemed very keen on guns and radio transmitters, but we assured them the bikes held neither and they let us go. We were stopped for papers twice before reaching our camp at Martil, but weren't delayed at all. Over dinner we discussed the financial situation, for once without acrimony, and Annie took over the management of our funds from Millie. The Martil campground was quite reasonable, with a reassuring wall and trees. The amenities block, however, had a broken tank on the roof, which led to cascades of water pouring down the walls and over the door. It was rather like walking under a waterfall into a river cave to brush your teeth.

Tetouan is the main tourist trap in the north, and catches all the day-trippers from Spain. We parked in the main square while Annie went to change some money, and were handed all the usual lines: 'I am from the tourist office. You are very fortunate, today there is the annual market, just one day. . . .' We had been told about this line, and assured that the market was not only on every day of the year, it also had prices especially inflated for the suckers. 'You want some dope? My father grows best quality. . . .' I get rid of these guys by quoting, with a straight face, a *Reader's Digest* story I once read on the horrors of 'the weed'. We had a lot of fun there in the square.

The road south through the Rif is lovely, with steep, scrubby hillsides reaching up to snowy peaks on both sides of it as it winds up to the plateau. After a stop to buy lunch at Chechaouen, a pretty little hill village, we pushed on towards Meknes—pushed on rather carefully, too, as the road was lined with some unpleasant car wrecks and we weren't keen to add a bike. The light was failing when we reached Meknes, and the politeness of a Moroccan bus driver nearly killed Annie and me. A lot of vehicles have a small green courtesy light affixed to the back, which they flash when the road ahead is clear. I took this bloke's word—or rather light—for it, but he was wrong. I made it back into the line of traffic with inches to spare.

Meknes has a most attractive campsite, with lush grass, gum trees, flower beds and stands of banana plants, all surrounded by the walls of the old sultan's palace. The lady with the 400/4 whom we'd met in France was here; she had teamed up with a chap on an XS750 which was currently a 500 twin—one cylinder stubbornly refused to fire. The army

Annie bargains for souvenirs in the spectacular Marrakesh bazaar. One of the great pleasures of visiting North Africa is the endless cheerful haggling

kept us awake that night with band and choir practice until the early hours. Sounded good, though.

The Meknes medina, or old town, isn't particularly exciting, but there's a good, versatile bazaar and most of the fruit and vegetables had marked prices. We indulged in a glass of the delicious mint tea that was to become our standard beverage in Morocco, and, luckily, didn't catch anything from the grubby hole-in-the-wall tea house. Just after our return to camp it snowed. The guards were delighted and told us that this was their first snow for 15 years. A lot of help that was to us, camped out in it! We'd had enough of the cold, and headed for the coast and then south.

Rabat was a very European sort of city, and at Casablanca we struck the only bit of motorway in the country. Everyone really liked it—you could see that by the traffic, which consisted of everything from pedestrians through buggies to loaded camels. There was very little motorized traffic, which was just as well, as it would probably have disturbed the people living under the bridges.

After a night in a nasty campsite at Mohammedia, which seemed to be inhabited solely by rapacious cats—one chewed its way into most of our dried soups—we pushed on to Essaouira. As we were rolling south through the rather dull countryside, I plotted a way in which I could attend my own wake. I would organize it when I got back to Australia ... amazing what idle minds will turn to. The campground was pleasant and run by a bloke who looked like an ASIO (Australian Security and Intelligence Organization) spook in his shades and jungle jacket. Farther south of here it became noticeably drier, and the goats had to climb trees to get at edible bits of greenery. We stopped to photograph some of them and became embroiled in an elaborate arrangement as to how much to pay which of the herdboys who clustered around. 'Whose goats are

If you look very carefully, you can just see a bit of Vetter top-box peering out of this Moroccan market crowd

113

those?'—'Yes, yes!'—'No, *whose* goats are *those*?'—'Yes, one dirham, yes!'

There is an abrupt rocky drop to sea level along this road that reminded me of Eucla on the Nullarbor plain. We stopped to chat with some surfies, who reported some tent slashing and stealing in their impromptu beach camp, but who were much more interested in how the swell was farther north. Disappointing, we told them. Flat.

We stayed at the campsite in Agadir, mostly because it had hot showers, and spent Christmas Day sitting around the pool, drinking beer and wondering what the poor people were doing. Agadir is a tourist resort like any other, with the same hotels and conducted tours, and didn't hold much for us, so we went south to the edge of the desert at Tiznit and then out along the dirt road 'piste' to Sidi Moussa. Along this stretch there was a bridge with a prominent 'detour' sign pointing down into the sandy river bed. Being good law-abiding citizens, we toiled through the deep sand with the bikes only to see a loaded truck go past on the bridge. Such is life. Sidi Moussa turned out to be a grimy, derelict place with one campsite covered in rocks and another deep in the sand, all inhabited by dubious-looking Europeans drawing on funny cigarettes.

As the war had closed all the roads, we could go no farther south, so it was unanimously decided to go back and spend some time in Essaouira. On the way, we were pulled over by police, who just wanted to have a look at the bikes, and one of them allowed that he wouldn't mind an XS1100 himself, but his BMW was so simple to repair that it was more sensible in Morocco. His friend looked familiar, and I soon realized that he could have been a rather slimmer Idi Amin. Lo! how the mighty are fallen. ... Rolling into the Essaouira campsite, we were just behind another Australian couple, Michael and Cathy Mol, aboard a BMW

Among the local arts and crafts for sale in this Moroccan up-country market are the water containers in the foreground—made from truck tyres cut and nailed together

R100S. They camped with us and we all employed ourselves lazing about in the sun. They joined us for the New Year's Eve fire on the beach, too, and Cathy absorbed a little too much of the local rough red wine. Being a gentleman, I won't go into details, but Michael had his hands full for a while. They were both a lot of fun.

Time passed quickly, as it often does when you're doing nothing, and we spent a lot of time just wandering around the harbour and fortifications of the town, which had once been a Portuguese trading post and had the cannons to prove it. The gates to the medina were still defended by bulky bronze mortars, now serving as rubbish bins. Freshly grilled sardines, straight from the boats, were an attraction on the wharf. One group of campers was permanently stoned, and it took them four hours to collect their meagre belongings when they left. They then wandered vaguely off in different directions. I guess they got a lift, because we didn't see them again.

The campsite, 'defended' by seven dogs augmented by four pups, became a home from home to us. One evening, a little fat-tyred 125 Suzuki fun bike rolled in. The occupants eyed the XS1100, R100S and GS750 parked near our tents and the lady asked, diffidently, 'Do any of you know anything about motorbikes?' We allowed that we did, just a little, and asked what was wrong. It turned out that the tiny bike would only rev out to $2\frac{1}{2}$ thousand, and then died. My first suspicion was the sparkplug, because I'd had similar problems with my XL, but it wasn't that, as we found out when we unbolted the carburettor float bowl. This was filled with what looked like fat white worms. The rider then remembered that he'd had a petrol leak from the lip of the bowl, and put sealing compound on it and bolted it back in place. He must have used a whole tube, because the stuff had squeezed out and set in the bowl, forming

Wherever you go, kids are fascinated by motorcycles. Michael and Cathy keep an eye on the bikes while the rest of us go shopping in this little village high in the Moroccan Atlas

the worms and stopping the float from moving. The bike had been like this for 1000 miles, they told us. I hope they made it home to Switzerland.

Annie got an abscess on a tooth and had to go to the local dentist. Although she claimed afterwards that he had been quite good, her heartrending screams under treatment suggested differently. The chap was so concerned about hurting her that he waived most of his fee. There's a tip there.... The Yamaha's battery ran flat, too. Mind you, we had been tapping it for our fluorescent camping light for ten days without running the engine—not entirely recommended. I was grateful for the accessory kickstarter, because pushstarting didn't work and this way we could run some improvised jump leads from the BMW while I kicked—the leads wouldn't carry enough current to use the electric starter.

The fine weather broke towards the middle of January and we moved on to Marrakesh and more blue skies. The Mols came with us, and it felt like a bike club run with the three bikes. Camp was made in the larger and cheaper of the two rocky Marrakesh sites and although hygiene left something to be desired, it was a relaxed sort of place and we settled in well. Marrakesh was like something out of the *Thousand and One Nights*. The old main square, the Djeema el Fna, was filled with conjurers, fire-eaters, snake charmers, dentists, acrobats, musicians and traders at all hours of the day. The intricate passageways of the souks, the markets, held fascinating workshops and good bargains—if you haggled carefully. We left the bikes outside in the care of the human parking meters, attendants with large brass plaques which they wore proudly and ostentatiously. You had to bargain with them, too, over the parking fees. Our most spectacular coup came in the campsite. An old bloke was selling warm, fuzzy, striped blankets, and he had one that was really lovely. His starting price was 350 dirhams, and he assured us that was not his 'rich tourists price'. After an entire evening of dedicated haggling, he settled for 35 dirhams, a t-shirt, two pairs of socks, a shirt, a tie and ... one of Annie's bras. He had a little trouble figuring out what this wispy nylon thing was, but he got the idea when we held it onto his chest. Then he was hugely amused.

In town, we found warm showers, in a hamam (bathhouse) next to the Regent Cinema. The first warm showers for a month, and you could stay under them for as long as you liked. Ah, luxury. The Mols, Annie and I spent one evening on a café balcony overlooking the Djeema el Fna, watching the trading and performing going on below us by the light of pressure lanterns. When we got back to the bikes, we were overwhelmed by a crowd of little boys, perhaps five years old on average, who, like a locust swarm, proceeded to pick our pockets and climb all over us and the bikes. They disappeared like smoke when a soldier came along. It was just as well, for how do you defend yourself against five-year-olds?

Annie and I took the Yamaha up to the pass leading inland over the Atlas, to see if it was possible to get across to Ourzazate. The road was mostly clear, and where there was snow or ice on the surface the truck drivers had been spreading gravel. So the caravan moved on over Tichka

Pass and down into the western margins of the Sahara. The Atlas is quite lovely here, with sheer rock flanks and tiny stone villages, all shrouded in snow. We stopped in Taddert for tea and were bombarded with demands that we buy handfuls of the sparkling crystals found around there, but we managed to resist the temptation. Just over the pass there was a bus lying by the side of the road—it had taken a corner too wide and rolled three times. Although the casualties had been taken away, we could still see the rust-brown stains of blood on the broken window glass—a chilling reminder to ride carefully.

Ourzazate boasted a basic but comfortable campsite—it had running water and a helpful caretaker-cum-guard, who looked after us to the extent of making a fire in a tin and preparing tea for everyone on it. There was also a good market and a much-detested Club Mediterranée. The people resented the place because it bought nothing from them.

We pushed on north along the flanks of the Atlas, over narrow and often broken desert roads but it felt like the real desert, with very little vegetation and occasional small herds of camels or goats. At El Kelaa an old man in a torn djellaba came up to us and started extolling the virtues of sidecars in a mixture of French, German and Arabic. He had fought in the Second World War on the side of the Germans and they, he told us, had had sidecars with *machine guns* on them! And the British had come over in aeroplanes, shooting, and the French had shot him in the leg. Oh dear, what a lot of fun the war had been . . . he sounded just like the old soldiers back home.

The Ksar es Souk campsite had deep grass and trees but very little water. We had also run out of gas for our stove, and small bottles were unobtainable, so we ate sandwiches. Later, someone told us that there was a spring just outside town where there was plenty of water and free camping, as well as palm leaves to make a fire. Ah, well.

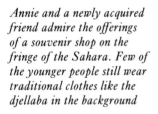

Annie and a newly acquired friend admire the offerings of a souvenir shop on the fringe of the Sahara. Few of the younger people still wear traditional clothes like the djellaba in the background

On the way back up into the mountains we had almost alpine scenery up to the Col du Zad, where we had a snowball fight. After that it looked more like the end of the world. With a high plateau, bare and windswept, with snowdrifts huddling against black rock piles, this was one of the grimmest places I'd ever seen. It went on for quite a few miles, the road snowploughed clear to one car's width, and we felt the cold creeping in even under our Alaskan suits. The plateau ended very abruptly and the road dropped through pine forests to the very French resort town of Ifrane.

The alleys of the Fes bazaar are still alive with the old traditions, such as these religious buskers with their pole of veils

A few miles later, over good roads, we were in Fes, the new part of which looked very French, too, but the old town was straight out of the Dark Ages, with its narrow, convoluted, noisy passageways. We actually employed a guide—the first time I'd ever done that—and it was just as well, even though he was more interested in taking us to his friend's shops than showing us the town. We would never have found our way out alone. The next day was my birthday, and I was presented with a cake and then sixteen buses loaded with 600 Danish schoolchildren invaded the camp. They came in the morning and left in the evening without ever looking at the town. A mystery.

We took advantage of the ridiculously low postage charges to send our souvenirs home and had the parcel wrapped very professionally by the semi-official parcel wrapper at the post office. He had a folder full of letters of appreciation from past customers, which he insisted we peruse while he wrapped.

After arranging to meet us again in Athens, the Mols took their leave to return to England and we turned towards the Algerian border. After an oil and filter change by the side of the road we rode past Taza, pretty on its hilltop, up to a famous cave in the mountains. The steps leading down were in woeful condition and when I saw a photo of it in London months later, it revealed 'Bon courage' scribbled on the wall of the cave near the bottom. It had been too dark to see this cheerful note while we were down there. We camped in the showground at Taza, watched by an inquisitive donkey, which then tried to steal our food and threatened to bite when chased off.

There was no problem about obtaining Algerian visas at Oujda, near the border, except that we had arrived on one of the innumerable Muslim holidays, so off to the border and the only campsite, to wait for three days and, in the café, watch the worst TV programmes we'd ever seen. I

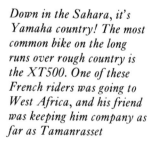

Down in the Sahara, it's Yamaha country! The most common bike on the long runs over rough country is the XT500. One of these French riders was going to West Africa, and his friend was keeping him company as far as Tamanrasset

had a nasty bout of 'flu, and lay in the tent drugged to the eyeballs while tempers again deteriorated around me. I didn't help by snapping at anyone who came near me. In the end I got fed up with it all and suggested we split up as soon as we were out of the desert.

When the consulate finally reopened, one of the questions on the visa application form was 'Will you be sufficient during your stay in Algeria?' The bloke opposite me grinned and said, 'I guess the only answer to that is "Quite",' so that's what we put down. Insurance was much cheaper than it had been at the Moroccan border and we were processed quite

Market day at El Golea way down in the Sahara. You'd better like spring onions and carrots down here—because that's practically all you can buy

quickly, but then the 'route rapide' on the map turned out to be the 'road slow', because it was less than half finished and we got to Tlemcen tired and dirty. It took ages to find the campground; none of the locals seemed to know it existed, but when we did find it it was comfortable and free—the only real drawback was a watchdog that delighted in untying people's shoelaces and chewing through tent ropes. I collapsed again as soon as the tents were up, still feeling rather ill, and things started getting heated again. Neil insisted that we split up right there and then. He was right, too—if it isn't working, don't drag out the agony. We slept on it, and I think he was a little surprised when I started sorting out the gear in the morning. We divided the equipment and Annie and I, on a rather overloaded bike, set off down into the Sahara. By ourselves.

Feeling very much at peace with the world, we buzzed across northern Algeria, with a short stop for coffee, on into the greening countryside. Spring was in the air, people waved to us and we swept around the tolerably well-surfaced twisting roads in a thoroughly good mood.

Then half the gear we had balanced precariously on the back of the bike fell off—we lost our spare visors, Annie's shoes and some food, but we weren't particularly perturbed. Even the obstinacy of the police in Tiaret and Songeur didn't bother us much. The tourist office had assured us that these worthies would point out places to camp where there were no official sites, but all they would do was direct us to a hotel. 'You are rich Europeans, you can afford it.' Pleas of antipodean poverty fell on deaf ears. A farmer just outside Songeur was considerably more helpful; not only was he glad to offer us a place to sleep, but he supplied us with milk and eggs and refused to take any payment. The whole family cheered us as we rode away in the morning. Algeria was turning out to be a much more hospitable place than it had been painted in Morocco.

It was getting noticeably drier now, and as we neared Laghouat we entered the desert proper. Vegetation, which had been scarce for 100 miles or so, disappeared completely and so did the few flocks of goats and sheep; only the camels remained. Shops became scarce, too, in the few towns we saw and we found it difficult to buy bread. Annie finally got some in a restaurant in Laghouat. The roads weren't bad, but the frequent detours through deep sand were rather trying. The bike handled them well considering it was now loaded up with all our camping gear, food reserves and 30 litres of fuel and water, although the sand was still a strain. We were glad to see Ghardaia, our first real oasis, and its jolly but expensive campsite.

One French traveller had a copy of the Fabulous Michelin 135—the map of the Sahara crossing that's been out of print and totally unobtainable for years—so I borrowed it and made a few notes in my diary; then it was on to El Golea. The desert scenery, which was flat, without hills or dunes, and with rock-covered sand to the horizon was rapidly becoming boring. The one bit of relief on this leg was an enormous golfball on an even more enormous tee just before El Golea—it turned into a microwave repeater when we got close. There was more flatness the next day on the way down to Ain Salah. I was a bit worried about the road surface before lunch, but a meal made all the difference and I relaxed in the afternoon. Food is an excellent medicine for the jitters.

The truckies down in the desert were painfully polite, and they would pull off the narrow tar when they saw us coming. The only problem was that they would then throw up an impenetrable screen of dust, which hid the road, so you never knew if there was another truck behind the first, in which case we would have been decorating his radiator. 'Where did you get the flat motorbike motif, Abdul?' 'It just came to me one day. ...' The bike returned nearly 49mpg (Imp) on this leg, the best it did on the entire trip, which was a testament to the flatness of the Sahara, but the road was full of shallow potholes, no more than an inch deep, which I learnt to ignore.

Ain Salah was a strange town; built of mud, or concrete covered with mud, it sat in the desert like a low rock outcrop. Aside from a half-dozen lackadaisical cafés, it seemed to lack shops, even the markets selling only oranges and carrots. Despite its isolation—it must be just about in the middle of the desert—Ain Salah is a cosmopolitan place; I guess they get all types coming through. We were warned not to camp in the

The markets in Tunis are rather better supplied than the country ones, and the fruit and vegetables are excellent. Annie tries to make sense out of yet another currency

'palmeries', the palm plantations, because of the mosquitoes. They got us anyway, despite the fact that we sought out a little stand of palms in the middle of the sands; Annie returned to the tent with a badly bitten bottom after answering the call of nature. We held a council of war the next morning, and decided to turn back. There is only one road down through the desert and you must return the way you came. That would have meant looking at the same flat nothingness for an extra three or four days, and we decided we'd rather spend the time somewhere more exciting.

The little palm-line campsite in El Golea sheltered us for a while, and we explored this huge oasis and its surroundings—Annie even tried out the bathhouse, but wasn't impressed. One afternoon, a Land-Rover with two Australian ladies aboard rolled up. One of them got out and said, 'Geez, I'd give my *soul* for a cold beer.' We directed them to the one 'good' hotel in town.

Our return to Ghardaia was uneventful—more sand and rocks—and we had a look around this "second Mecca", so called because parts of the valley are still closed to non-Muslims. Then we set off for El Oued and the Tunisian border, and rode straight into the teeth of a sandstorm. By the time we had turned east it had become a crosswind and was throwing the fully laden bike all over the road—on one memorable occasion, even into the sand. Coupled with the limited visibility of about 20ft it was too much for me and we turned around.

The most excruciatingly boring day followed as we sat in the tent and listened to the wind howling outside. After the third game of Scrabble we just sat there and stared at the canvas. But it had settled down the next morning and we made good time across—you guessed it—more flat desert. But near El Oued the country changed and soon we were riding through, and sometimes over, enormous sand dunes. This was the Great Western Erg, the sandy desert you see in the movies. By the side of the road, the telegraph wires often disappeared into the tops of dunes, only to reappear on the other side. Reception must be awful. We also saw date palms and herds of camels, and decided that this was much more like it. Why couldn't the whole Sahara look like this?

When we reached Hazoua, a Tunisian border post, a slight problem emerged. The tourist bureau leaflet had assured us that visas were issued at the border, but the border guards thought otherwise. 'Not possible.' A pretty pickle. We couldn't go back, as our Algerian visas had been cancelled a few minutes earlier at the Algerian border, and we couldn't go forward. We couldn't really stay there, either. Without money-changing facilities or a shop, Hazoua didn't really make it as a campsite.

One of the skills you develop if you travel a lot is knowing when to shout and when to whisper and I decided this was a shouting situation, so I waved my press card and introduction at them. The latter, from *Middle East Travel Magazine*, was in Arabic and impressed the guard sufficiently for him to get on the radio. He came back and said, perhaps, but it would take three days. We sat down to wait. I was fairly confident they wouldn't let us starve. A hectic night was had by all. The guards were nervous and afraid of the Lybians, who had attacked the nearby town of Gafsa a few weeks earlier, and they spent the night prowling around with loaded guns and flashlights. We slept in the Customs post, more afraid of those guns than of the Lybians. A false alarm involving a Belgian camper van lightened the atmosphere a little as the terrified Belgians were dragged in at gunpoint and interrogated. We got very little sleep.

Things looked better in the morning. The Chef du Poste arrived and cut through some of the red tape, and we were finally on our way at noon—following the local bus, which was carrying one of the guards and our passports; the visas needed duty stamps, which were obtainable only in the next town. We were to meet the guard there, pay for the stamps and get our passports back. There was one more hurdle, however, in the form of a police checkpoint just outside town. The bus was checked and went on. Then it was our turn. As I tried to explain in my school French that the passports the cop wanted to see were on the bus, he became more and more annoyed and began to toy with his sidearm. Fortunately, the guard on the bus remembered us round about then and came back. He was abused for inefficiency by the cop, who then let us pass with a big, toothy grin.

Tunisia didn't really turn out to be worth all the trouble. We rode up to the coast at Nabeul through uninspiring country, camped and went in to Tunis to pick up mail and book the ferry to Sicily, and Annie scouted out a replacement gas bottle for our stove, which was a relief. Nice to be able to do your own cooking. We moved to a hotel in Tunis, because the ferry left at 6.30am and the nearest campsite was two hours from the

'An unassuming little mint tea, but with a fine nose....' Taking a break at Essaouira, Morocco

port. The Hotel Medina was nice; our hosts insisted that we park in the lobby, which I'd intended to do anyway. Then we went out and bought some English newspapers as well as paté, salami and bread, and had a feast of eating and reading in our room. We explored the medina as well, and found it pretty if a little tame, discovered the excellent produce markets and then slept until 5am. Then the alarm on Annie's little calculator, the desk clerk and the muezzin from the nearby mosque woke us simultaneously.

Getting the bike into the hotel lobby had been easy with a dozen helping hands, but now that it was just Annie, the desk clerk and me it wasn't quite so easy to get it out. After a 36-point turn, scuffing their paintwork with my front tyre on every one, I managed it and we rode off down to the ferry. While we were waiting in the light, sprinkling rain for them to open the gates, an XS500 arrived ... then an XL125 ... then two bicycles. I kept expecting someone on a skate board .... After an elaborate check of papers, which failed to turn up the fact that we had overstayed our visas, and a confused Customs check, we finally rolled aboard. Back to Europe!

Chapter 10

There are roads—and roads

Sicily to Greece

Sicilian roads could do with a bit of work, as this stretch above Catania will testify. The XS1100 handled these conditions very well, despite being ridiculously overloaded

THE FERRY TO Trapani wasn't exactly the QE2, but it got us there; everything was rather shabby and the bar and restaurant were expensive and generally closed. In the third class saloon, where we made our home for the 12 hours of the crossing, there was strict segregation—the Arabs sat on one side, we Europeans on the other. The curious thing was that you didn't actually see this division happen—it just developed. When we first sat down, there was an Arab family sitting near us, then, as more Europeans arrived and sat on our side, they moved. We spent most of the crossing playing cards with the French guys riding the bikes we'd met at the gate. True to form, these two let me struggle along in my idiot French until they wanted to explain something about the game we were playing—and then they suddenly spoke passable English. The French are hilarious; they always do that.

The Immigration check in Sicily must have been carefully designed for the absolute minimum in efficiency, but the Customs check that followed was considerably keener—it involved our first encounter with drug-sniffing dogs. One of them, a cheerful hyperactive German Shepherd, was much more interested in chewing our tentpoles than in looking for drugs. I politely asked the handler to restrain his beast. Then it was out into the chilly, wet evening and up the autostrada to Palermo. Sicily in the failing light was almost unbearably picturesque, although I'm sure I would have enjoyed it more had I been warm and dry. We reached the 'Pepsi Cola' campsite just as it was closing and the padrone took us into the office and poured us a brandy before we got down to the formalities. Sicilians are very perceptive people.

It dawned wet and cold, so we inserted ourselves into our Alaskan suits and MCB boots—waterproof boots are a real blessing when you get several days of rain—and went exploring. The site watchman warned us to beware of pickpockets in Palermo, but apart from the post office giving us change in stamps rather than cash we weren't robbed.

Northern Sicily is a rugged place, with awe-inspiring cliffs sheltering long ranges of hills like overstuffed pillows, with a fine needlework of vineyards embroidered on them. Despite the drizzle, we had an enjoyable few days exploring. Every now and then the padrone back at camp would get worried about us and offer us alternative accommodation—first it was a little wooden house, then a caravan. All free of charge. He couldn't understand that we were quite happy in our tent.

As the skies looked clearer to the south, we finally packed, had a last cup of coffee in our little bar on the harbour and headed across the island to Selinunte. We rode through seemingly endless fields of yellow flowers and discovered a peculiar system of motorways. These roads weren't on our map, and seemed almost like miniatures—a proper motorway scaled down to Fiat 500 size. Altogether in poor repair, the system didn't seem to lead anywhere, and I had some vague memory of the fascists undertaking construction programmes in economically depressed parts of Sicily; this could well have been one of them. A chap we met along the way showed us a rather eerie place to have our picnic lunch—the main square of Gibellina, a town destroyed by an earthquake in 1968 and never rebuilt. We were stopped by the police a little later, but our total inability to speak Italian foiled them and they let us go. I've found that ignorance is generally bliss when talking to cops.

The Greek temple at Selinunte was in better condition than most of the ones in Greece itself, but the campsite that had been recommended to us didn't seem to exist. We carried on to Sciacca, through endless rows of holiday houses in various stages of incompletion and invariable poor taste. The sun came out, and in the morning we were served excellent Espresso coffee right at our tent. A great institution, the waiter-service campsite. As Caltanisetta's bypass road wasn't quite finished, we had to go through the town itself. This is the one environment in which a heavily loaded XS1100 really doesn't shine. The narrow, cobbled streets with their sharp corners gave me quite a bit to do. An additional problem is that you can't get yourself out of trouble with the throttle—there's nowhere for the bike to go if you accelerate. We were caught in a Communist Party march as well, which slowed us down even more. Caltanisetta had good ice-cream though.

Down past Enna, we took the spectacular autostrada, which just ignores the lie of the land. When it isn't swinging itself over the valleys on a 'viadotto' it's drilling through the hills in a tunnel. It must have cost an absolute fortune to build.

On the coast once again, this time the eastern one, we found a supposedly closed campground called 'Bahia del Silenzio' at Brucoli, which opened just for us. With typical kindness, the people offered us a small bungalow, but we stuck with the old tent. We'd finally woken up to the most economical way to supply ourselves with wine, and bought a 5-litre plastic container, which we regularly refilled with the local vintage, just like the Italians do. After a quick look at Neapolis with its amphitheatre, near Syracuse, we turned north once more, to Catania. The inland road looked good on the map and turned out to be quite exciting, with steep hills and ridgetop runs, but on the way back down it became a little too exciting when we hit a sizeable patch of diesel and went sideways for a little while. No damage, but a bit of heavy breathing and cursing resulted.

A very thorough tour of Catania then, helped by the motorway signs, which pointed around in a large circle, taking in most of the town. We both got really annoyed with this and rode around swearing at the top of our voices until at last the autostrada entry ramp came into view. Fortunately, the Italian motorway cafés serve excellent coffee. We recovered our composure over cappuchino. Camp was at Acireale, just north of Catania, in a clifftop campsite that had a lift running down to the beach. Talk about luxury. Another sort-out left us with quite a bit of gear to mail home, and we parcelled it all up neatly and took it up to the post office. It wasn't to be that simple, though. First of all, I hadn't left enough loose string for them to put their metal seal on. They retied the parcel for me. Then, I hadn't put a return address on it. I tried to tell them that I certainly didn't want the parcel returned to the campsite, but it seemed that a return address was required by law. So I put the same address on the parcel twice, which made them very unhappy, but they took it. Losing a little weight made the bike look much neater.

We rode up around Mount Etna, through hazelnut plantations and past pretty little towns balanced on hilltops, and on north through a national park and a vast hunting reserve. Lovely country up here, with some excellent road over the passes that took us to Milazzo and a German-run campsite called, inexplicably, 'Sayonara'. The weather was pleasant, but the locals still seemed to find it wintry. At a petrol stop on the way to Messina, the attendant came out of his office shaking his head, pointing to the bike and crying 'Freddo! Freddo!', which I took to mean 'cold' in Italian.

The Villa d' Este near Rome boasts hundreds of fountains—some of them very unusual indeed

The ferry to San Giovanni on the toe of Italy was quick and cheap. They had excellent coffee on the ferry, once again, and nice pastries, but the signposting out of San Giovanni reminded us unpleasantly of Catania. When we finally made it out of town, we rode up the coast through Scylla (Charybdis must have given up monstering, it wasn't to be seen) and on north. People seemed rather offhand and not particularly friendly, even suspicious. When we tried to change some money at an airport, the teller regretted that the bank had run out of money. Fruit and vegetables didn't seem as fresh as those in Sicily, and the roads were worse. We really didn't think much of southern Italy . . . there was a lovely campsite in an olive grove at Lamezia Terme, admittedly. We took to the auto-strada to get us north—it's free as far as Salerno—and we followed it up through the southern mountains, past occasional snow patches, with our warm clothes, heated handlebar grips and GloGloves on. The hills were lovely, with only occasional factories polluting the air.

Naples welcomed us with its expensive but invaluable 'tangentiale' ring road, which we followed to its western end to a campground that had been highly praised. The site featured a swimming pool fed by a hot spring, and we spent as much time in the water as possible. The city itself was a disappointment—it seemed to be little more than a permanent traffic jam; we were glad to get out. Pompeii was the real attraction and we spent some satisfying hours there. With a little imagination, the town comes alive just as it was before the ashes of Vesuvius swallowed it. Annie and I also looked through the creepy underground ruins at Cumae, with their huge trapezoidal tunnels. On a lighter note, we bought a little chess set and I discovered to my delight that I could actually beat Annie. Only because she hadn't played before. . . . Neil and Millie were there, too, both looking well. They had had a little trouble with the GS in the desert when one of the carburettors had jammed and drained the petrol tank in less than 40 miles, without their noticing. The locals had helped them.

We rode up to Rome in bright sunshine by way of Cassino and the Via Appia, picked up our mail and found the 'Roma' campsite without any trouble. Along the way, we discovered that the intricate Rome one-way system doesn't apply to bikes. You can ride anywhere you like, in any direction. At one point we scattered the crowds around the Trevi fountain. There were lots of fellow Australasians at the camp, and we spent most evenings standing around the fire drinking beer and telling lies. Because we'd taken the bike off to be serviced, we had to use public transport for getting around. This consisted mostly of buses like enormous green tin sheds on wheels, which are free. Well, they *do* have a ticket machine, but the only people who seemed to use it were the nuns. Nobody ever appeared to check for tickets. We visited the Colosseum and the Capitoline Hill, which was inhabited by a great tribe of tough-looking cats. The catacombs were closed, allegedly for renovation. For us, the highlight was the Vatican Museum. Not so much for the Sistine Chapel, which looks and feels like an ecclesiastical railway station, but for the superb ethnological section.

With the bike back on the road, though not greatly improved by Italian servicing, we took in the more remote spots like the Villa d'Este, with its hundreds of fountains, and Hadrian's villa. One night, the Goodyear blimp put on a brilliant lightshow over the city. While we sat on a park bench craning our necks, moving coppered pictures flitted across the sky—we were entranced.

Before departing for Umbria we bought some new clothes, which was a real luxury after living in the same very limited range of clothing for so long. Our first stop was Assisi, with its houses of honey-coloured stone stacked one on top of the other on the hillside and a quiet campsite overlooking it all. The tomb of St Francis, deep in the rock, was very impressive. We had some pleasant sunshine, but it was still cold in the shade—as I discovered when I washed my one and only jacket.

It was wet and windy again on the road to Florence and we were forced to fortify ourselves frequently with coffee and cakes. Having arrived, we decided to cop out for once and stay in a *pension*. We were sick of the rain and wanted to feel warm, clean and human for a change. Punishment came, of course—someone broke into the topbox and stole our airbed pump. I had locked the steering, put the alarm and the massive Abus lock on as well as covering the bike with the Vetter cover, but all to no avail. We didn't do too badly, all things considered. The pump was the only thing stolen on the entire trip. Our *pension* was comfortable, with *en-suite* bathroom featuring a working hot shower and central heating. A little time was spent outside—we looked at the Ponte Vecchio, wandered the streets drooling at the shop windows and toured the Uffizi gallery. I become very easily overloaded when confronted with too much art in one stroke, and emerged shellshocked. Annie coped much better. Then it was back out into the rain and off to the mountains and the snow, but the road over to the east coast had been freshly cleared; it was empty of traffic and fun on the bike. We rode up the mountain to San Marino with the big motor enjoying the work. Hills were never a problem for the Yamaha and I very rarely even had to change down.

San Marino was a real, genuine tourist trap of the first order—a gem of a rip-off. The only good value was booze, so we stocked up. It was cold, too, and we huddled in our sleeping bag waiting for the morning, which brought a dullish run to Venice, where we installed ourselves in the Treviso campsite.

Venice repays the effort made to get away from the main tourist haunts; there's a wealth of interest in the backstreets and alleys, and coffee is cheaper, too. Perhaps the place is a little too devoted to chasing the lire, but it's none the less interesting for all that. All the dogs wear muzzles, by the way, although some of them have their pacifiers just slung casually around their necks without interfering with the use of the teeth at all. Very Italian. I felt inspired that night—perhaps Venice had kindled a fire in my soul—and excelled myself at dinner, even if I do say so myself. With only two pots and one flame I produced hamburgers, mashed potatoes with onions and mushrooms in white sauce. Didn't taste too bad either. . . .

Yugoslav roads demand infinite patience. This is a stretch of the main Titograd–Skopje highway—and it's not one of the worst bits

Italy had seemed tame to us after the rigours of North Africa, so we were rather looking forward to Yugoslavia. We didn't have long to wait before things got rigorous again. At the border, the official took one look at our pretty blue Australian passports, went into a huddle with his pals and then disappeared indoors, where he got on the telephone, looking worried, leaving us sitting in the drizzle without an explanation. All I could think of was that there had been some reports of terrorist training camps for an anti-government right-wing organization called Ustashi in Australia. Perhaps the border police thought we were Ustashi shock-troops. Eventually they decided to take a chance and let us in.

On to Zagreb with a will, through pretty country with the first flush of spring on it and the last clouds of winter above it, but one of Zagreb's alleged campsites had disappeared, the other was closed—so were most of the cheap hotels. We checked into a reasonably comfortable place near the railway station and went out to do the town, but the grim weather made that a rather uncomfortable pursuit, so we retired early and wrote letters. We had intended to devote a day to the famous Plitvice lakes south of Zagreb. The rain became heavier and colder as we rode out of town, and the bike began to run rough and lose power. I pulled into a petrol station in Slunj and took the fairing off. The problem wasn't difficult to trace—one of the plug leads had come undone and been casually pushed back, which I can only presume had happened during the service in Rome. It was soon fixed and gave no more trouble, which is more than I can say for the Yugoslav weather.

When we got to the lakes the rain turned to sleet, so we decided to get the hell out of there and down to the coast. Then, naturally, I got lost. The bloke behind the counter of a hardware/booze shop gave us directions. It seemed like an odd range of stock for a shop, but the more I thought about it, the more sense it made. . . . Back on the main road, I overtook a truck without realizing that there was a dip in the road ahead; the dip, of course, held a car coming the other way—the big Yamaha dived off the side of the road quite gracefully, I thought. Annie's opinion was otherwise. The bloke in the car just shook his head. We recovered with a terrific meal of roast pork and chips in Otocac and washed it down with a brandy before tackling the godforsaken plateau above Senj. It snowed again on the pass, but then we were through the weather and rolled down the twisting mountain road to the sea and sunshine.

We found a sweet little campsite on the water and it was actually warm enough to eat dinner outside the tent, although not quite warm enough for a dip. The rain came back the next day as we rolled into Dubrovnik and we couldn't resist the offer of a *pension* with a garage. A German couple touring on an elderly BMW R60 joined us and we spent most of the evening telling stories over a few drinks. A lot of Germans seem to speak English, which is handy. A few days in Dubrovnik were a real pleasure. We did all the usual things—walks through the medieval city, around the walls and out to the fortress, as well as familiarizing ourselves with Yugoslav cooking. There was a small bar tucked away in an alley down by the harbour that specialized in burek, the cheese or meat pastry.

133

They also had cevapcici and raszkici (grilled meats) and we spent every evening there having a few beers with dinner.

An absolutely horrifying detour through the mountains claimed us as soon as we left Dubrovnik. The 'road' was a more or less recently graded dirt track, and over the 40 or so kilometres it lasted we counted three trucks that had fallen off the side; two of them were lying on their sides, and one had rolled over onto its roof. The bike dealt with the surface quite well, due no doubt largely to the fat rear tyre, but there was chaos at the other end as cars and trucks squeezed past each other on the narrow cliff path. We were more than glad to be on the bike.

Just before Titograd we fell foul of a radar trap. For once, I actually had not been speeding, but you can't argue with Yugoslav traffic cops. They just snarl at you. I paid the fine and rode on, seething. Still, if they caught me every time I *do* exceed the speed limit.... The Titograd campground had been vandalized badly since Charlie and I had stayed there 18 months before. The pretty lady wasn't in reception, either—in fact, there wasn't anybody in reception. I finally found someone at the hotel that adjoins the site and they told me to camp anywhere I liked, the site was open and free. Annie thought they just couldn't be bothered filling in all the forms. The watchman came past, cadged a couple of drinks, and promised to look after our tent extra carefully. I went to the

If you look very carefully, you'll see that this Greek delivery trike does actually have a motor

bank to cash a cheque and had to scribble my name on it four times before the teller was satisfied that my signature matched the sample.

Then on into darkest Yugoslavia, up hill and down dale on steadily worsening roads. We took the main road, not the track that Charlie and I had taken, but at times it wasn't much better. Winter had destroyed more than one bridge and undermined the road so often it was like a trials stage. In one tunnel there were great ice pillars, formed by water dripping from the ceiling, but we made it through to Skopje and then over quite passable back roads to Ohrid. We heard a sad story that night in a cevapcici bar, where we were having dinner. A young Yugoslav soldier came over to us and introduced himself in fluent Australian. He had been taken to Australia by his parents when he was five years old and had lived in Canberra for 16 years. Then he'd come back to see his relations and the army had grabbed him for two years' national service. He had eight months to go, and was counting the days. Our landlady gave us a heroic breakfast, including a gallon of coffee. Annie had washed her knickers and hung them on the back of the bike to dry, something we often did with wet clothes, and the landlady nearly cracked up. She thought it was the funniest thing she'd ever seen, and called out all the neighbours to share her glee.

The people at Bitola were helpful and pointed out the road to Greece, which was just as well as there wasn't a single road sign in the whole town. There were money-changing problems at the border—never change more money than you need—and the obstinate Greek Customs man wrote the bike into *my* passport, which was near to being full, instead of Annie's, which had more space. But you couldn't really stay annoyed long. The spring was with us—it had been following us all the way from Sicily, and now it was finally catching up.

After a run through fresh greenery we made camp at Meteora, below the famous rock cliffs like stone trolls with monasteries for hats. We watched the tourist buses rolling up, and it struck me as odd that the monks should be able to reconcile the religious life with showing tourists around all day. Do they pray for a good tourist crop in between counting the admission money, I wonder? There was a large chrome and glass establishment in Kalabaka which advertised itself, in large day-glo letters, as a 'typical Greek taverna'. Yeah, sure. Annie was befriended by a little black dog we nicknamed The Sheik for his habit of creeping into our tent when we were asleep. He followed her devotedly everywhere she went. The proprietor of the site didn't know who owned him. 'He just likes tourists,' he told us.

The Plain of Thessaly, although it sounds good, was dull. The excitement set in on the mountain road after Lamia, where a new road was being built and the old one had been sort of lost underneath, making it pretty rugged.

After passing the great olive grove of Itea, we climbed the cliff to Delphi and camped right on the edge of the drop. The scramble around the ruins was well worth it, but it's best timed for when the tourists are at lunch. Delphi is one of the prime sightseeing spots in the country and becomes badly crowded even in the off season. We chatted to an elderly, tubby cop who was quite obviously in the grip of a lengthy love affair with his Harley Davidson. He showed us where he'd painted this ante-diluvian monster himself, careful dabs of the brush over rust patches. A German arrived in the campsite one night on a shiny new BMW R45, still in shock from travelling on the Lamia road. We told him to try the Skopje–Titograd highway if he wanted a real experience. He was cheerfully horrified when he saw us loading the bike, and asked politely if he might take pictures.

The road to Thebes was fine, except that the surface deteriorated badly whenever we went through a town. Often town streets were dirt, perhaps the powers that be feel that it's a waste of time tarring them—they'd only wear out again anyway.... The motorway was silly, with lots of 60-km/h restrictions, and we were caught once more by the radar. This time I wasn't going to put up with any nonsense, and anyway I'm not scared of Greeks the way I am of Yugoslavs. I pointed out, at the top of my voice, that I had not been doing 135 as they claimed, but only 100, and anyway didn't they have anything better to do. Annie joined in with my tirade and they practically shooed us away, dazed by our combined assault. We later found out that the speed limit was 90.

Athens was, as always, dusty and noisy, with cancerous traffic. We picked up some mail, including a pair of visors from Bob Heath and a note from the Mols saying that they'd be joining us a week later. That night, we were overcharged for our dinner of calamari down in Piraeus, and the waiter plied us with free retsina when we complained—we felt that we were getting this travelling business pretty well sorted out.

The week until Michael and Cathy arrived was spent exploring the Peloponnese. A couple of days lying in the sun at Epidaurus with an excursion to the well-preserved amphitheatre were followed by a visit to Sparta. Then we headed over the ranges to Kalamata and ran into more snow. It really is true; you become much more sensitive to nature's little quirks on a bike....

On Easter Sunday, the proprietor of the 'Melbourne' café in Hora bought us some cakes and coffee. People kept giving us Easter presents all day—boiled eggs dyed red, biscuits and even a cucumber were thrust into our hands by people standing beside the road. Everyone was out in their front yards, roasting lambs on spits; the countryside smelt like a vast Greek restaurant. Olympia, which we'd intended to make the high spot of our day, had been closed by a strike. Back to reality! On the tollway back to Athens, the toll collectors in their little hut waved us through for free, but it wasn't a good Easter for everyone. As we crested a hill, a puppy wandered out onto the roadway. I made a crash stop and Annie scooped it up, but its owners weren't to be seen. It had obviously been abandoned. We stood by the side of the road for a while holding it up as we'd seen people in Morocco do who wanted to sell pups, but nobody stopped. A puppy isn't a terribly sensible companion on a bike trip, especially when you have to cross borders. We really didn't know what to do. Finally, we took it along until we reached the outskirts of

Athens, found a prosperous-looking suburb and dumped it on someone's front lawn. We assumed that its chances would be better there than on the motorway. But as we drew away, it was already tottering back out onto the road. A sad end to Easter, both for the pup and us.

We set up camp, bought some wine and sat around feeling miserable. The next day we had trouble at the bank and begrudged the Bulgarians their extortionate fee for a 30-hour visa. A pall descended that wasn't broken until the Mols arrived, grinning from ear to ear.

Chapter 11

'Your bike has just turned turtle . . .'

Athens to London

Annie, Cathy and Michael inspect the Dardanelles ferry in Turkey with rather bemused looks. This wasn't the one we caught—ours was smaller, and it didn't have the fences down the side

MICHAEL AND CATHY had left London in the cold and drizzling rain, and had had much the same weather until southern Germany, when the snow had started. On the autobahn to Austria, they had been riding through snow drifts and had camped in them in Salzburg. Finally out of the heavy weather on the Yugoslav coast, they had had a slight argument with a large, pointed rock which had bent their front rim and flattened the tyre. Michael had bashed the wheel back into shape with his axe, replaced the tube and they'd ridden on. And they were cheerful when they arrived in Athens! We rolled out the plastic jug of retsina and sat down for a little party. It was good to see them again. The hangovers in the morning were something to behold, except for Annie. She's the only person I know who knows her limit—most of the time anyway. We packed up rather gingerly and then flew up the motorway. None of the speed traps were interested in us. The strain of keeping up with the R100S showed on the Yamaha's worn-out shock absorbers, and I wallowed around the corners the BMW was taking in style.

The weather was deteriorating again, but we got away from it by spending a couple of days on Thasos. This island is less than an hour from the mainland by ferry and specializes in honey and having its roads sink into the sea. It's a pretty, pine-covered place and has a good campsite as well as miles of coastline suitable for free camping. We had a barbecue on the beach, using a suntan lotion rack as a griddle, and sank a few beers. Then it was time for a run around the island, checking out the sunken roads—there were several places where you could have gone skindiving without leaving the saddle—and back to the mainland. On the way up to Alexandropoulis, over those pretty mountain roads, a police car came the other way around a corner while I was way over the centre line—they didn't bat an eye as I corrected and drew sparks from my centre-stand.

The rack on the XS had developed a couple of cracks in North Africa when we had overloaded it so badly, and these were getting worse. Reluctantly, I decided we wouldn't be able to carry spare petrol in Turkey.

We had another game of hunt-the-gasbottle for our little cooker. You can buy the cartridges everywhere, and you can generally buy large caravan-size bottles, but the little ones are hard to find. A cab driver finally took us around the town looking for one, for free, and found it. A knowledge of German is invaluable in Greece and Turkey, as so many people worked in Germany. Our cab driver, for instance, had saved enough money there to buy his cab.

The road to the border was indifferent and the service on the Greek side quick if not exactly courteous. The Turks were working at their usual pace—dead slow—and held us up for a while, but at least there weren't any Customs searches. The road down towards Gallipoli was initially quite good and for a while I thought we were in the wrong country, but it soon deteriorated, and the Mols took flying lessons on a tricky humpbacked bridge. We had lunch there and a German couple, he on an XS1100, she on a CX500, stopped and told us that a few years earlier they had managed to get a 4CV Renault airborne on that bridge. We had intended to have a look at the site of the infamous Gallipoli landings of the First Great Unpleasantness, but couldn't find any cliffs that looked likely. Later we found out that the landings hadn't been at Gallipoli at all, but on the other side of the peninsula. No wonder it was a disaster.

The ferry to Canakkale in Asia Minor had just left when we arrived at the wharf—it was only running intermittently due to a diesel shortage—so we were facing a three-and-a-half-hour wait. A man at the wharf told us about a local ferry that ran from a place a little farther down the coast; I wish he hadn't tried to help. This local ferry was a mildly converted

Although there was a petrol shortage in Turkey, that wasn't the main problem. There was an electricity shortage as well, and pumps had to be cranked by hand ...

fishing boat, with extremely flimsy rails and nothing to tie the bikes to. We shared it with a defunct tractor and a van, and it was so crowded that the bikes were right on the edge. We hung onto them for grim death all the way across the Dardanelles. It would have taken only one largish wave. . . .

Past rows of closed campsites—the season hadn't started in Turkey—we rode to Troy for a look at the ruins. The place is quite a mess. Apparently there are numerous Troys one above the other and it's all a bit of a chore sorting it out. It is very impressive, though, to see several thousand years of civilization in a few yards of hillside. You'll be glad to know that the wooden horse is still there. You can even climb up inside and play Greeks and Trojans. On the way back to the main road, a kid lobbed a rock at us. My feelings, about this kind of thing haven't changed since the first time it happened in Afghanistan. I turned around and went back—with the motor on the red line in first. The kid ran as though all the demons in hell were after him, and I guess the big Yamaha sounded a bit like that. I caught him and gave him a dressing down in front of his mates. Lots of pretty hill country then, and a tiny campsite marked 'Kampink—Piknik'. It was quite idyllic, but they'd run out of beer. I guess no place is ever perfect.

The BBC World Service news was cheerful and informed us that three people had died in political shootings in Turkey during the day. I'm glad to say that nobody has ever shot at me—well, not for a good long time, anyway—and nobody shot at any of us in Turkey. We had to search for a while before finding a petrol station that would give us juice the next morning, not because there was a shortage of petrol but because the electricity was off. Not all stations have hand pumps.

The road to Izmir reminded me of Greece. As soon as you got into the town limits, the tar stopped and the gravel started. After Izmir we were on the main road again and diced with the buses and trucks down past Ephesus to the coast at Kusadasi. The town is a port of call for many of the cruise liners that ply the Mediterranean and prices in town go up between 100 and 2000 per cent whenever ships are in port. We learnt to do our shopping after they had left. There were some pretty bike leathers for sale here and I was tempted, but they weren't that much cheaper than in Britain, and you get after-sale service in Britain. We lay in the sun for a bit, and I bolted the stays from the top box onto the bike frame instead of the rack. Not quite so elegant, but it put less strain on the cracks.

Going inland, we followed the country lanes for a while, riding through the little villages dozing in the sun, before we returned to the main road and the traffic. At Pamukkale, an area of hot springs and calcium deposits that turn whole hillsides white, we camped in a tiny site with a large pool. The pool was bigger than the camping area. Our host was a keen man after a buck, as a lot of Turks are, and we had an interesting run-in with him. Michael priced the beer, an essential step if you don't want to find yourself with enormous bills. He was quoted 40 lire for a bottle. We both hit the roof, as 30 is considered expensive, and our genial host backpedalled rapidly. 'Oh, you want the beer for *drinking*! That's only 30.' Hmmm. The frogs in the pool did their best to keep us awake and there was an attempt to short-change us in the morning, but, other than that, Pamukkale was a pleasant place. On the way out of town the clutch on the BMW started slipping quite badly, but Michael adjusted it up as far as possible and managed to make the bike rideable.

The road we had selected to take us back to the coast was marked as 'stabilized' beyond the little town of Kale on our map. In Kale, we stopped for a glass of tea and Annie and Cathy were the only women in the tea house. We donned rain gear, and the locals tried to dissuade us from going on. 'Rocks *this* big and mud *that* deep!' they said. They were right, too. 'Stabilized' turned out to mean deep, gluey mud and we lasted a little more than a mile before deciding it wasn't for us. That road was 56 miles long! Our alternative was better, and a filling lunch of köfte (meatballs) and beans was enlivened by a conversation with a couple of bank tellers, who were delighted to exercise their English. They told us that petrol prices had doubled in the previous month. We still thought it cheap.

On the road down through the ranges, Michael suddenly pulled over to the left and stopped. I followed, put the side stand down—and the bike fell over on the slope. The stand had broken through the tar, and the bike tipped, spilling Annie and me off—right under the back wheel of the BMW. Now Michael had pulled over because he thought he smelled something burning. His first thought, therefore, when I dived under the back of his bike, was that I was putting out a fire. So he dived off as well, also ready to extinguish the blaze. Confusion reigned for a minute until we had it all sorted out, the XS back on its wheels and Michael reassured that the R100 wasn't about to go up in smoke. Annie then saved the day by producing the brandy flask. Those Vetter fairings really are good—better than any crashbar. There wasn't a scratch on the XS.

We found a campsite out at Kemer, past Antalya—it was free because the season hadn't started—and we did a bit more lying around in the sun, as well as going for a run down the coast to Kas. This stretch was as pretty as ever with its steep, pine-covered hills and empty beaches. The road that was being built when Charlie and I had come through here a year and a half before was already disintegrating. The Yamaha handled the potholes and gravel noticeably better than the BMW. The BMW also had a flat tyre on the morning of our departure. Nothing to do with Turkey, this was an after-effect of the encounter with the rock in Yugoslavia. The tyre had sustained a slight split on the inside, and this had been plucking away at the tube, finally tearing it. I'll say this for BMW, they supply an excellent pump.

After another ethnic lunch at Antalya, we rolled east along the rather featureless coast. In Anamur, the bikes were parked on an embankment above the market square while we did some shopping, but suddenly a gust of wind caught the BMW and flipped it onto its side. The bike landed right on the edge of the embankment, slipped over and crashed down a foot and a half onto its back on concrete. Then it tipped onto its side. Almost a complete somersault. At first it looked as though the only damage was a broken mirror and a cracked fairing, but when we tried to ride away the back tyre was rubbing against the guard. The fall had bent the rear frame loop. Fortunately, another campsite presented itself just down on the beach. When the owner realized that we were having problems with the bike, he invited us to dinner and drinks. A thoroughly drunken night followed: we tried to teach our host some Australian songs; he recited a great deal of poetry, we did some dancing; there were drunken protestations of eternal friendship; and I gave two guys a lift home on the bike—both of them on the back at the same time. Annie misjudged the strength of the raki and went to sleep in my lap, and what finally saved us was the shop running out of raki. We had to switch to the considerably less alcoholic beer. I've seldom had such a good time.

We 'repaired' the R100S in the morning with a couple of borrowed crowbars, took a look at the marvellous Crusader castle while our hangovers abated and then tackled the cliff road east. This is a great run through stunning country, made less pleasant only by the lumbering timber trucks. We had trouble keeping up with the flying Mols as the BMW's handling came into its own. Camp was at the BP Mocamp that Charlie and I had disliked so heartily on the previous occasion. Everyone wanted a shower. The place was still as expensive and the staff as rude

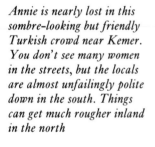

Annie is nearly lost in this sombre-looking but friendly Turkish crowd near Kemer. You don't see many women in the streets, but the locals are almost unfailingly polite down in the south. Things can get much rougher inland in the north

143

as before, but at least the water was hot. Then on to Mersin, where a tractor tried to run Michael off the road, and up through the Cilician Gates to the Anatolian Plateau. The dual carriageway claimed by our map turned out to be sheer optimism—all they'd done was make the old road *less* passable with their roadworks.

The Rock House Hotel at Göreme was closed, perhaps because it was still early in the season, so we went to 'Paris' Camping instead, which not only had hot showers but free gas cookers and tables and chairs. A few days passed pleasantly enough with sightseeing and clambering in and out of stone houses, and we changed the rear tyre on the XS without any of the problems experienced by the bike shop in France. Getting the bead on the tyre to pop properly wasn't easy with only a hand pump, though, but the security bolts gave no trouble at all.

We climbed to the top of the stone fortress at Uchisar, and one of the town urchins chased us all the way up with a guide book. Unfortunately, he'd gone by the bikes—German registration on the Yamaha and German tax-free registration on the BMW—and had brought the German guidebook; a wasted climb.

On the way to Ankara via Kirsehir everything was green again. The fields and meadows were feeling the spring even here on the high plateau. Crossing an embankment, the Mols hit a pothole and bombed the unsuspecting peasants below with one of their panniers—the Krauser came off the bike, bounced along the road and then dived down into the

A restaurant just made for a bear! That sign is actually supposed to be English, and reads 'Beer, Wine drink— Roast meat—meal of meat and sweets—Fish'

144

fields, but there was no damage beyond a few scratches. The main road to Ankara hadn't improved since I'd last travelled it and we had to contend with long stretches of gravel and dirt. The Ankara campground had taken down its sign, but I remembered where it was and we managed to wake the guard. Although my old friend Rochester had gone, we were still not allowed to camp on the grass—just like old times. When we went off to do a little shopping, we discovered that a kilo of onions cost the same as $6\frac{1}{3}$ bottles of beer. There's a moral there somewhere.

It was back out into the grey air and heavy traffic of Ankara in the morning. Martial law was in operation, every corner had its soldiers, and at strategic intersections there were rows of tanks. The tank crews were really taken with the bikes and waved enthusiastically as we passed. We waved back, of course.

The BMW started to lose oil rapidly, and it didn't take long to find out why. The sump was gradually lowering itself on its bolts and spitting out oil. Michael tightened it, making ominous comments about Turkey and BMWs. Then we were off to do battle with the traffic on the Istanbul road. The less said about this run the better—we were forced off the road once each and didn't really enjoy it. The first tanks at the outskirts of Istanbul were actually a welcome sight. Soon afterwards, we rolled over the toll bridge back into Europe. We located the most convenient camping ground, set up the tents and ducked off to town for dinner; I took the others to the little kebab bar Charlie and I had found, where the food was as good as ever. We resealed the sump on the R100S with liquid gasket and I put the stays from the top box back into their proper place on the rack. I thought we were through the worst of the roads; little did I know.

After the obligatory rounds of sightseeing, which are more worthwhile in Istanbul than in most places, we raided the Grand Bazaar. It sells everything from everywhere—all at negotiable prices. Never believe what the merchants tell you, just dig in and enjoy it. They have some beautiful things—I bought Annie a miniature painting on ivory and myself a pipe. The radio featured marvellous selections from sixties and seventies rock as well as classical music, and we played a chess championship. I won! But only because all the others were even more of beginners than I. An idyllic existence, despite martial law and shootings.

One night, in a so-called pub, we were watching some execrable TV when a chap walked up, introduced himself as a sailor who had been to Australia and offered to buy us a drink. Thinking of the grim roads we would have to cope with on the way back to camp, we declined. He looked at us in disbelief and said: 'What part of Australia are *you* from?' Then the Mols were off again to southern Greece and the sun, carrying with them our Scrabble set as a farewell gift. We turned our wheels towards Bulgaria and then home. The trip had lasted over six months by this stage and we were quite happy to have it end. A tour has a sort of natural lifespan, although most people have to get back to work before it runs for that long. The lifespan of our tour was coming to an end, and it was time to let it die gracefully.

The Customs man at the Bulgarian border asked us for third-party insurance, which we no longer had. When I told him this, he rolled his eyes heavenwards and waved us through—he couldn't be bothered getting the forms out. Bulgarian roads were pretty nasty, mostly cobblestoned and wavier than the Bay of Biscay in a gale. We felt our way gingerly through the forested hills to Veliko Tarnovo. The campsite there turned out to be the most expensive of the trip, but at least they had plenty of hot water for the showers, although I cannot for the life of me imagine why the taps were electrified. . . . Perhaps some of the cost of the site was an entertainment charge. We were certainly entertained, by singing and revelry, until about 4.30am. We were glad to get out of

Michael and Cathy climb down from the lobby of the Rock House Hotel where Charlie and I had stayed during our visit to Göreme. The volcanic rock is quite soft and easily carved

Bulgaria after our extensive stay of 24 hours. Among other things, the roads had finally done what even the Yugoslav ones had not managed—they had broken the rack.

Romanian Customs must have had us pegged as International Drug Runners. They searched everything on and off the bike, even though their drug-sniffing dog didn't show the slightest interest in us. We then had to change $10 per day of our visit into the local currency and should also, apparently, have bought petrol coupons. Nobody told us anything about them, so we rode blithely off. As it turned out, only one petrol station asked for them, and they filled our tank anyway when we shrugged our shoulders. The roads were noticeably better than the ones in Bulgaria, and we made it to Bucharest for lunch. We ate at the Carul cu Bere, a restaurant in an 18th-century inn. The food here was superb, beer came in great stoneware steins and was delicious, and it was all quite cheap.

It was frustrating trying to find somewhere to camp. Most of the sites listed in the official booklet (another damned official booklet) were either closed or had disappeared. One was even closed for stocktaking! 'One tree, check. Grass, 80 square metres, check. Pile of gravel. Where's the pile of gravel, Karoly?'

When we finally found a site the bike immediately attracted a crowd of truck drivers. While they were admiring the twin disc brakes up front, one drew me aside. He told me that he was Hungarian, and to be sure to lock everything up. The Romanians, it seemed, were all *thieves*. Marvellous, I thought. Why do neighbours always delight in blackening each other's names? This slanderous tendency isn't restricted to Hungarians. When I made a disparaging remark about the Bulgarian roads, all the Romanians were tickled. One of them pointed to the dirt track we were on and suggested that that was what the Bulgarian roads were like. I said no, worse, and he pointed to the ploughed field next to the campsite. When I nodded, they roared with laughter and then bought us a beer.

We had a race with a diesel locomotive up into the Transylvanian Alps and lost when we came to a red light. These mountains are beautiful and full of old châteaux and grand hotels from the days before Communism. Most of them are workers' holiday hostels now—one improvement, anyway.

Somewhere in the north of Romania we lost the rubber plug out of the cam chain tensioner. I manufactured a new one from rolled-up adhesive tape and wired it into place—it seemed to do the job very nicely. We were once again trying to find a replacement gas bottle, and in Oradea near the Hungarian border finally found a gas depot. It was closed, but there were some people outside and one of them took our empty bottle, passed it through the fence and got a new one back for us, free of charge. Nice people everywhere.

The border with Hungary was easy, except that once again we had trouble changing unwanted money back. Because it's against the law to take Romanian money out of the country they wouldn't give us anything else, and we had to spend our remaining cash on souvenirs. The roads to

Budapest were smooth and straight and almost unbelievably flat. With conservative and polite drivers as well, Hungary is one of the most pleasant countries in Europe to ride in, although things weren't quite so easy in Budapest.

Annie checked with the Tourist Bureau and they told her that the campsite was closed, which seemed a bit unlikely to us. We rode out there just to make sure and lo!, not only was it open, but it was open the whole year round, and it was a pleasant enough site despite the loud disco music from the restaurant at night. Isn't it great to see Western culture spread behind the Iron Curtain? Budapest has excellent public transport and is an altogether prosperous city. The people still don't look happy though, and the truckloads of Russian soldiers we saw were pointedly ignored.

We took the road along the Danube on our way to the Austrian border and were rewarded by quiet country lanes and lush greenery. The border was quick as they were only searching cars, not bikes. As we rode into Vienna that afternoon, the back wheel of the Yamaha started making the most peculiar scraping noise. I tracked it down to a shoelace caught in the rear brake caliper.

Old BMWs are much prized in Turkey. This specimen ran like a clock

An overnight stay in Vienna, in a clean and well-equipped campsite, and we were on our way again—no more time for sightseeing. The border with Germany is a one-stop affair—they showed our passports to a computer, which raised no objections, and we were simultaneously out and in. Coming in to Passau, we started chatting to a bloke on an ancient BMW outfit, and he showed us a good pub for lunch. We camped in Nuremberg that night, near the stadium made famous by the big Nazi rallies. It's a parking lot now, which seems appropriate. The campsite was excellent, as all German campsites seem to be. Then it was up the Autobahn, on to Brunswick and a few days with relatives. Then a long day across to Ostend and the late ferry to Dover. Due to delays on the ferry—it kept yo-yoing around in Dover harbour—and problems with the ramp, we didn't get ashore until well after midnight. The Customs man asked us where we'd been and wasn't at all impressed by the 18 countries I rattled off. He just asked whether we'd picked up any 'noxious substances' and when we said no, we didn't think so, let us go.

Miracles do still happen. There was a bed-and-breakfast place still open on the Folkestone road, and the first thing our landlady did was offer us a cup of tea. We were back in England, all right.

The run to London was just a formality. We were back, 194 days, 20,000 miles and £2000 after we'd set out. A great trip.

Chapter 12

Full dress for the road

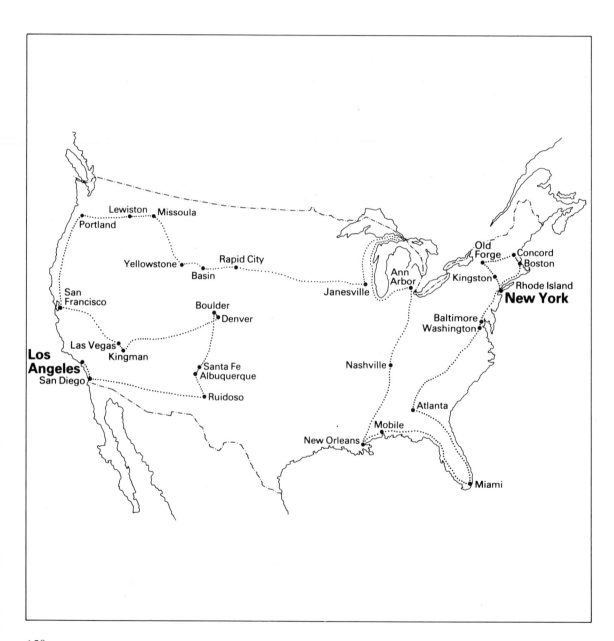

The American approach

TO MANY RIDERS outside the United States, all the Americans ever contributed to motorcycle touring was the Harley Davidson Electra Glide—and a lot of European riders reckon we'd be no worse off without it! The Milwaukee Monster seems to embody the soul of American touring for riders in Europe and to be the antithesis of what they believe motorcycling is all about. As such it represents the dichotomy between the different approaches to motorcycling in general and touring in particular on both sides of the Atlantic. Europeans generally prefer their motorcycles to be light, responsive, easy to flick from side to side through a series of bends, stable, well braked and powerful. The bike should become an extension of the rider's senses, with rider and machine functioning as a single entity, rather than being a separate mechanical device on which the rider must sit in order to operate the controls. This attitude is changing as a new generation of riders emerges in Europe, weaned on the Japanese bikes of the seventies, ready to accept compromised handling and roadholding because they have never experienced anything better. But it does explain the European predilection for café racers, BMWs, Ducatis, Laverdas and Moto Guzzis. It also explains why heavy Japanese machines such as the Gold Wing and the Z1300 were slow to take off in Europe.

In Europe, if a rider has a Ducati 900, a BMW R100S, an Egli Kawasaki or a Morini 350 and he wants to go touring he simply straps a tank bag to the bike, maybe adds some throw-over soft panniers, bungees a soft bag to the pillion or carrier, and off he goes into the wild blue yonder. In America, the market seems to have developed along different lines. The guy or girl with a Ducati 900 or Moto Guzzi Le Mans is a sports rider, a street rider or a café racer. Seen from across the Atlantic, the American touring rider is a different kind of animal, easily identifiable by a full-dress kit including copious fairing, saddlebags, tail trunk, touring saddle, probably a CB radio, possibly a stereo radio/cassette player, and maybe even another 30 add-on items that convert a perfectly adequate motorcycle into a grotesque touring rig. That's the European myth; how does it match the Stateside reality?

Like most generalizations this one isn't quite accurate because the picture is simply not that black and white. When I was riding in the US I met or saw several riders out touring on fairly standard machines, but they were far outweighed by the full-dress set. I even had a cheery wave from a guy riding the other way down Interstate 10 on a Gold Wing that was dwarfed by, and almost hidden behind, a vast fairing carrying no less than four headlamps in line abreast across its snout! When The Bear travelled coast-to-coast across the United States (see Chapter 13) most of the riders he spoke to were surprised to find him tackling such a trip on a trail bike, and when British journalist Annie Briggs of *Motor Cycle Weekly* rode from Atlanta, Georgia, to Ruidoso in New Mexico for the 1978 Aspencade Motorcycle Convention most riders thought she was nuts to travel all that way without so much as a fairing for protection. While a small minority of American motorcyclists happily go touring on Italian sports bikes, naked Triumph Bonnevilles or chopped Harley Sportsters, the majority do their touring behind large fairings with their belongings carefully stowed in saddlebags and tail trunks behind them. Cubic inches have always been important to Americans, whether on two wheels or four, and although the recession of 1979/80 has seen touring equipment cropping up on a lot of smaller bikes, the most popular mounts for touring are undoubtedly the Electra Glide, the new Tour Glide, the Honda Gold Wing and the larger BMWs.

Europeans have been scornful of American riders' preference for some time now. That's not so much the fault of the Americans; it was just that whenever Europeans complained about various shortcomings of Japanese machines to the manufacturers the answer always came back that market research showed that was how the Americans wanted it. The US

BMWs are among the best touring bikes in the world, and the R100RT may well be the best of the bunch. I rode this model from Los Angeles to El Centro before being hit by a severe case of strep throat, but recovered to ride south of the border into Mexico at Nogales where this picture was taken

market in the seventies dominated the marketing plans of the Japanese Big Four, so when Europeans moaned about too-small fuel tanks, tyres and disc brakes that didn't work in the wet, rusting silencers, ignition systems that converted fours to twins in wet weather, skimpy mudguards, too many idiot lights and a number of other problems we had to blame either American tastes or the myth that it never rains in Southern California. And when the popular Honda 400/4 was dropped by the factory we were told it was because it wasn't selling too well in America. A lot of European enthusiasts were left with the feeling that American riders didn't know what motorcycling was all about and, furthermore, were lousing it up for those of us who did!

Things weren't all bad, though. For a start, the European market became increasingly important. Handling, brakes and tyres started to improve; Honda even started making certain models for Europe only, such as the CB900FZ, and others for America only, such as the CB900 shaft. The Gold Wing was designed to capture the lion's share of the growing American touring market from Harley-Davidson and BMW. Honda didn't care if it wasn't an instant success in Europe because the factory knew it could sell economic quantities of the 600lb beast in the United States. The Wing was a runaway winner Stateside, offering new standards of reliability, civility, noise control, power and comfort to the touring rider. Its success spawned the Yamaha XS750 and XS1100, Suzuki GS850 and GS1000 shaft, the Kawasaki Z1300 and ultimately

Peter Rae, then editor of Motorcycle Rider *magazine, and Cyril Ayton, editor of* Motorcycle Sport *magazine, found it their turn to be on the other side of the lens when they were snapped by a passing local BMW rider on the road from Tucson to Nogales*

the Honda CX500. Today these are among the best touring bikes available anywhere, on either side of the Atlantic. The Japanese had discovered the drive-shaft and given touring riders everywhere rational alternatives to the highly popular but very expensive BMW twins. It all happened because the Japanese factories found out that Americans like to travel long distances on big bikes—so perhaps Harley-Davidson sparked the whole thing off in the first place!

What amazes Europeans is not so much the bikes—the Gold Wing and the XS1100 are now big sellers in Europe—but what the Americans do to them after purchase. Americans are accessory nuts! *Road Rider*, the leading touring magazine in the States and probably in the world, started featuring readers' bikes carrying the most bolt-on accessories back in 1977. Eventually they had to stop the feature because things were 'getting out of hand', but before they did they included a 500 Honda four owned by Bruce Mayer from Escondido, California, which carried no fewer than 38 items. The list included floorboards, fairing, cigarette lighter, 'dashboard', 'glove compartment', CB radio, FM stereo radio, eight-track tape deck, four added tail lights, extra mirrors and triple crash bars around the saddlebags. Overkill? Not for Bruce Mayer, and presumably not if your primary interest lies in fitting accessories rather than riding motorcycles. The art of 'dressing' a touring motorcycle in America now seems to have become an end in itself, just as happened years ago with choppers and more recently with the rebirth of the café racer. Unfortunately when customizing reaches this stage the results can be grotesque. No one in his right mind (me, intolerant?) is going to add giant front mudguards and reflectorized 'bumpers' around the saddlebags to an already overweight tourer such as a Gold Wing or Z1300. But folk do—not to mention chromed tailpipe extensions, several dozen tail

Aspencade is littered with full-dress Gold Wings, many of them with trailers—but few with canine friend in tow!

lights and handlebar tassles. I guess it's a matter of taste, but when it goes this far it's not mainline touring, it's exhibitionism.

The American craze for accessories has had a significant effect on touring world wide, however. Until the mid-1970s riders in Britain faced a very restricted choice when it came to touring bolt-ons. Fairings were almost exclusively in the 'sporting' mould, racks or carriers were often of poor quality and impractical design, Craven was virtually the sole supplier of top-boxes and panniers, and if you didn't get on with the standard saddle you had to change the bike.

But as motorcycling took off again in Britain and Europe, several enterprising souls started importing the best American goodies. The items were very expensive and the range limited at first, but before long British and European accessory manufacturers saw that time was running out for ugly 'universal fitment' products. Vetter and Calafia fairings and saddlebags arrived in Britain, and local manufacturers were not slow to bring out copies and look-alikes. The ubiquitous white gave way to colour-matched accessories, bike radios hit the market, and helmet intercoms appeared as if out of the blue. Suddenly everyone was making

The king of American touring but priced beyond the reach of most European riders: the Harley-Davidson FLH Classic

tank bags, replacement touring saddles, leather, plastic and glass–fibre panniers, low-level exhaust systems, racks and tote bags. Prices started fairly high and are still rising, but now in 1982 you can hardly find a completely standard motorcycle on the streets of London. Again, we have the Americans to thank.

So far the excesses of American taste have been avoided among Europe's touring customizers. The peculiar penchant for towing trailers or campers behind solo motorcycles is rare in continental Europe and unknown in the United Kingdom, where it's illegal. The British Motorcyclists Federation is currently trying to persuade its government to change the law and allow the towing of trailers, not in response to any groundswell of opinion among touring riders in favour of trailers but because the government automatically assumes such combinations to be 'dangerous and unstable' despite the lack of any evidence to support or destroy this theory from US experience. Even if it is made legal I don't think you'll catch many British riders taking to trailers as Americans have done. You simply don't need that much carrying capacity on a touring holiday, and a trailer would make a nonsense of the pleasures of motorcycling through the Alpine passes. Maybe that explains something of the different attitudes towards touring on either side of the Atlantic. America's 55mph speed limit turns its touring riders into cautious speeders with one eye permanently on the lookout for the police and the

Kawasaki's attempt at a mainstream tourer, the Z1300. Effective but still not as popular as H-D, BMW and Gold Wing

other flicking regularly towards the radar detector, or it forces them to cruise in the 55 to 65mph band, taking in the scenery and enjoying the on-bike entertainment. I was surprised a few years ago to see a survey of Gold Wing owners published in *Road Rider* where the average most comfortable cruising speed quoted by respondents was something like 64mph! I find the Wing most comfortable between 80 and 90, and I reckon it's rare for a European rider on a large machine to go touring anywhere at 64mph. The approach to touring may be different, but there's no question that if you're out there on the open road travelling from place to place on a motorcycle you're touring—whatever your speed, the size or make of you bike or the number or suitability of accessories fitted to it. In that most important respect there is real affinity between touring riders world wide.

The next few years should see far more intercontinental travel by touring motorcyclists, so each can sample the other's brand of touring at first hand. Transatlantic air fares are at an all-time low. A growing number of companies and organizations on both sides of the ocean are offering either complete touring packages by motorcycle or motorcycles for hire. Full details are given in the Appendix at the back of this book. American readers will have read already of the pleasure that awaits them on the roads of Europe. The Bear's account of his trip across the USA is bound to whet European appetites for a taste of touring American-style.

Aspencade is an annual affirmation of the health of the American motorcycle accessory manufacturing industry. It's also one of the friendliest rallies in the world

Chapter 13

'You came all this way on *that*?'

The XL during reassembly in New York. Something very heavy had been dropped on it during its trip across the Atlantic, and I had to straighten the shock absorbers with a crowbar....

Wasn't it religion that was supposed to be the people's drug?

New York to San Francisco

We were in brilliant sunlight at 30,000 feet as the Laker DC10 started its descent into John F. Kennedy Airport. Ten minutes later, on the ground, it was night—darkness broken only by the beacon of the dozens of aircraft milling around waiting to park or take off. I found myself hoping fervently that this was not going to be an omen for my long-awaited tour of the US. Half an hour later my fears were firming up. The immigration lines in the arrivals lounge were long, slow and staffed by people obviously bored with their job of keeping America safe for democracy. I got short shrift—two months to be precise—when I tried to get an entry permit to take me up to the date on my onward ticket—all of three weeks later than the two months.

But—America, land of contrasts!—things were quite different at Customs. Not only did the officer disdain to search my luggage, but as soon as he noticed that I was a motorcyclist—easily deduced from the crash helmet under my arm—he engaged me in a lengthy and interesting discussion of bike usage in the US. He then closed his station and went off to find out the easiest and cheapest way in which I might get my bike, which had come by air freight, out of bond. Ten minutes later, equipped with detailed—and unfortunately wrong—information, as well as the address and phone number of my first American friend, I boarded the bus into Gotham City. For $5 the airport bus is good value. You get to goggle out at the fascinating and scary concrete ribbons of the freeways, contemplate the towering housing projects and remember all the warnings about New York—while you're still safe. As soon as you step out of the bus at the Lower East Side Bus Terminal you're on your own. At 1am, for me, this seemed about on a par with crossing Parramatta Road (Sydney's main traffic artery) at 5pm on a Friday afternoon. Death lurked everywhere.

One of the taxi drivers—a sizeable black person—lent me a dime to ring the Youth Hostel. They didn't answer, so I decided to go round and wake them up. The loan of ten cents had put me so much in the moral debt of my driver that I didn't feel able to protest his charge of $8.50 for ten city blocks. ... He did me a favour by pointing out that I was in one of the toughest neighbourhoods in Manhattan, and to watch out. If anyone tried to put trouble on me, he suggested I keep walking. I amended that to 'running' and thanked him. The hostel was closed, of course, but I got a room in the hotel next door, as well as a much-appreciated snack in the hotel coffee shop. The bell boy pointed out that the TV would operate only if the bathroom light was switched on; I gave him a dollar and fell into bed.

I am a creature of sunshine. The next morning, with temperatures climbing towards the century mark they reached every day I was in New York, I felt immeasurably better and more in control. I checked in to the hostel, stowed my baggage and went out for a walk. As I left the hostel, my eye was caught by the unmistakable shape of the Empire State Building, visible through a gap between some other buildings across the road. I stopped and admired it for a moment, then turned and walked on. 'Hey, buddy.' A well-dressed black bloke standing in a doorway marked 'NY Community College' called me over. 'Buddy, I been workin' here for 20 years. Ever' now and then, folk stop where you did an' look up in the air. What you lookin' at?' I motioned for him to come back a few steps with me, to where he could see the Empire State, and pointed.

'The Empire State?' he said. 'Oh, *yeah*, *sure*. The Empire State. Yeah. Never thought o' that. . . .'

It was beginning to get muggy, even early in the morning, and I turned up towards Central Park. It's a blast walking through New York. I doubt that there's a more interesting place on Earth. And it's all the people; the diversity, the style, the craziness. In Central Park, this being summer, it was all hanging out. I have never seen so many scantily covered ample breasts and buttocks in my life—and most of them on wheels, too. Roller skates everywhere, people with radios clamped to their heads bopping, rolling, even dancing . . . and rippling—the males with muscles, the females with, er . . . other tissue.

The remainder of those couple of days is a bit of a blur. There was Greenwich Village, with the frisbee experts working out in Washington Square; the great food in the delis; the great comics pages the Sunday

My little 'Harley-Davidson' in full US Touring Trim, complete with Oxford Fairings windscreen, a welcome addition

papers serve up; the sight of miles and miles of smog from the top of the Empire State; Waylon Jennings at the Lone Star for $1 cover charge; and the terrible beer. I approached the beer scientifically. In the evening, I bought one can each of six different beers and retreated to the room I shared with a swarthy Frenchman and two melancholy Danes. As I listened to tales of touring the US and Canada by BMW—this from the Frenchman, who'd shipped his bike over and spent eight weeks buzzing around—I sampled the brews. They were all awful, without exception. Pale, flavourless and nearly non-alchoholic, they all tasted the same. Bad sign. One of the Danes explained his melancholia, too. He had, it seemed, been mugged. His papers, money and travellers' cheques had been taken—in Miami, of all places. I'd always thought of Miami as a sort of geriatric ante-room to a morgue, but it seemed street crime was a problem. For the Dane, anyway. His embassy, fortunately had come to the rescue. They had replaced his passport on the spot and had lent him some money.

With the mugging story still fresh in my mind, I descended into the subways to make my way out to suburban Jamaica to pick up the freight papers for the bike. Graffiti on the NY trains is of a very high standard, and the trains themselves are occasionally even air-conditioned. Papers in hand, I then presented myself at the freight depot. It seemed that some mud had been noticed under the guards on the bike, so the Department of Agriculture man had to be called. Foreign mud is a no-no. I sat around, gasping in the heat, for an hour or so until he came. After one look, he decided that he wasn't worried. I was then free to deal with the lady from Customs, who suspected everyone and everything—she gave me a hard time because my bike registration papers had expired, but finally relented.

So I had the bike back—rather bent, since someone had dropped a crate on it, but still my bike. I had to straighten the shock absorbers with

Navigation in the USA is by route numbers. If you know the route you want, you can't really get lost. But woe to you if you don't!

161

The sublime meeets the ridiculus on the lip of the Grand Canyon

In upper Michigan, I met John-from-Boulder, one of the many Americans who invited me to stay in their homes

a crowbar, but the rest of it wasn't too bad and went back together quite well. It wouldn't start, though; throwing away the contents of the float bowl and pushing finally did the trick. My grateful thanks to the guys at Seaboard World, who donated a tank of petrol and then pushed. I couldn't have done it without ya.

My first encounter with the freeway system, on the way back into Manhattan, wasn't reassuring. The signs are so cryptic. What do I know about 72nd Street? Signposting is all very local, unless you've memorized the route numbers. No denying that the freeways get you around at a great rate of knots, though. I was back at the hostel before I knew it. I fitted my lovely new Oxford Fairings windscreen out in the street, and attracted all sorts of loonies. One of them insisted on telling me the long, dreary and predictable story of the disintegration of his Gold Star BSA. With the bike locked to a light pole, I went out for another night on the town. Once again, there were no dire consequences in the morning because the American beer is simply too mild to cause hangovers. That morning saw me stuck on the freeway within minutes of leaving the hostel. There had been a downpour, and half the road was under water— the half going my way, of course. Finally, on the way out to upper New York state, the buildings gave way to greenery. All of New England turned out to be surprisingly lush, which was still new to me at this stage. New York looked rather as I'd imagined Louisiana.

I made my way north to Old Forge in the next few days. In Kingston, in the obligatory aluminium diner (run here by a Vietnamese family), I encountered 'Doc', the head of the town emergency services. This includes ambulance, fire brigade and rescue. He was an ex-Marine Colonel, and insisted on giving me an enormous Marines badge, a small

Down in Louisiana, you don't have to watch out for bears any more. You have to watch out for alligators instead!

American flag and a free breakfast. The hostel in Old Forge was equipped with a large group of bicycling Canadian nymphets, who entertained me splendidly during my stay. They even fed me.

My petrol tank, once broken in Malaysia and often repaired, had been cracked again during the flight. I had to glue it up once again after I had noticed petrol running down over the hot engine. I turned east then, to head for Vermont and later the coast. By now, I was learning to navigate by route numbers and had no trouble finding my way about. I picked up a bit of sunburn buzzing around the little lakes and extensive forests of New England, and didn't mind one bit. It was beautiful and serene country, bathed in sunlight—with just the occasional thunderstorm and downpour to keep it interesting.

Concord didn't impress me so much. The home of one of my very few heroes, Henry David Thoreau, it was far from the small town surrounded by forest that he described last century. Now, it was a particularly nasty urban sprawl, reminding me of nothing quite so much as of Bairnsdale in southern Victoria, probably my least favourite city after Brisbane. That night, after tightening the chain on the bike for the third time, I finally discovered a reasonably drinkable beer. It was called Molson's, came from Canada and at least had some flavour. Still no strength, though.

This was turning out to be a relaxed, lazy sort of swing through pretty countryside, rather different from the America I'd been led to expect. Even Boston, my first big city outside New York, seemed a laid-back place to me. I drifted through on the main roads, stopped for a cup of coffee at the Transportation Museum, and then carried on towards Cape Cod. A group of three Canadian bikers passed me and then stopped to have a look at the XL. In honour of America, I had dubbed it 'Hardly Davidson', and these blokes thought that was very funny. Mind you, they were on a Z750, a GS850 and a Z1000. They could afford to laugh.

Redwoods are not only tall and wide, they're also remarkably tough. When I walked around this tree, I found that it was more than half hollow

Tightening the chain becomes a rather common exercise—like twice a day sometimes. This time, it's in the birch forests of Minnesota

It was misty all the way out to Cape Cod, so I couldn't admire much scenery, but there was enough to admire by the side of the road, anyway. Everybody was having a garage sale—some of the stuff people were unloading really tempted me. There were a couple of Buddy Holly albums, for example, in near-perfect condition, for only $2 each. . . . Once at the Orleans, Massachusetts, hostel, I took the tank off the bike, scraped off the liquid gasket with which I'd tried to stop the leak, and reglued it with an arcylic glue, which seemed to do the trick.

Crossing the high bridge at Newport, Rhode Island, brought to mind the grace of the yachts during the Americas Cup, and the film 'Jazz on a Summer's Day', made here during one of the real Newport Jazz Festivals. We see so much of America on TV and in the movies that it's quite possible to feel nostalgic entering a town you've never been to.

On my way up to the hills of Connecticut I stopped off for some of the dreadful, gummy American bread. When I came out of the supermarket, the bike was leaking petrol once again. This time it came from the carburettor breather pipe. I whipped the float bowl off, bent the float down and reassembled the carburettor. No more leak. Some time later, I looked down to find that the tank had split again, and petrol was dribbling onto the engine once more. I stopped at a hardware store and bought a two-phase adhesive that contained, according to the box, 'real steel'. I wasn't going to have any more backchat from the bike. I glued up the tank and the tap, which was weeping very slightly, and gave the bike as complete an overhaul as I, with my severely limited mechanical ability, could; I didn't discover any further problems.

It was back to NY then to check for mail and amble around a little

What is it about XL250 sidestands that makes them break all the time? Could it be that I put twice as much weight on mine as it was designed to carry? Rapid repairs here in Rapid City

more. In the footsteps of Walt Whitman, I took the Staten Island ferry and was impressed by the Manhattan skyline from the water. Then I rang *Road Rider* magazine in California for the dates of the Aspencade Motorcycle Convention, a 'do' I had hoped to get to for years, and planned my trip across the USA. Very vaguely, I might add. I just knew I wanted to be in Ruidoso, New Mexico, on 1 October. That gave me some eight weeks.

Up and away then. Out through the Holland Tunnel the next morning, the bike was running rather rough. I had visions of breaking down in the tunnel—there's nowhere to park—and being fined vast sums of money. But the bike kept running, and as soon as I was out of the tunnel and switched off the headlight, the engine smoothed out. Aha! Middle-aged XL Disease, I thought. One of the symptoms is lack of electricity being generated, and the bike can't even run its pitiful headlight. Mechanical menopause approaching here. Then on down the ribbon of car yards, cheap motels and gas stations that is Highway One until I got

A fellow Australian met on the road. His name, believe it or not, is Robin Sparrow

167

This crossing of the Continental Divide was from west to east, on the way to Denver. Rarified air gave me an 'altitude high'

hopelessly lost in roadworks in Baltimore. A thoroughly depressing city, it sticks out in my mind for the obvious poverty and overwhelming friendliness of its mostly black population.

Washington provided the Smithsonian Institution, where I admired Buzz Aldrin's toothbrush and touched a piece of the moon; the Star Wars subway, very efficient and pretty; and drinks at Matt Kane's bar. This last proved to be the most interesting, as I had a few drinks with the pilot of Air Force One, the presidential jet, and listened to his Washington gossip. It's true, he gave me a book of Air Force One matches! Other than that Washington was not pleasant. For a national capital it's remarkably run down. Brothels and sex shops flourish within a couple of blocks of the White House, and there's an atmosphere of menace.

I rode up the Potomac, and then followed the line of the Chesapeake and Ohio Canal. This is now a national park and is maintained for walkers, canoeists and bicyclists. It seemed as though there were thousands of butterflies, all keen to commit suicide on my windscreen or legs. That night was my first camp. I'd finally run out of Youth Hostels. So of course I had a thunderstorm and nearly an inch of rain in three hours. Huddled in my little tent (I'd bought it for $10 from some Swiss blokes in the Gol-e-Sahra campsite in Tehran), I consoled myself with the thought that the enormous caravans and mobile homes parked all around would be far more likely to draw the lightning than my little XL. I

Roller bearing trees don't grow this high up ...
Yosemite Valley, California

finally fell asleep while the thunder was still muttering to itself over the Shenandoah Hills. Over breakfast, I got an explanation of the mysterious term 'scrapple' that had started to appear on menus. 'Wal,' said the chef, 'yo bile up various parts of the hawg, let it cool and then slahce an' frah it. . . .' I stuck to bacon and eggs, over easy.

The Blue Ridge Parkway was next, a bit of road every bit as pretty as its name. Parkways have no advertising on them, follow the contours of the land and are administered by the National Parks Service. This one follows the Blue Ridge Mountains for some 500 miles, all of it lovely, with the Appalachians rolling off to both sides like waves in an enormous, ancient slow ocean. The Morgans, from Danby, Pennsylvania, pulled up while I was trying to take a photo of the forests, and asked about my Australian number-plate. They also volunteered a beer and insisted that I take down their address and come and stay next time I was around Danby. I accepted gladly. Americans are certainly a friendly lot, rather like the Irish, and much more friendly than the British or Australians.

Although I didn't see any of the bears that supposedly inhabit the park, I felt quite ridiculously happy all day, sang little songs and waved at all the Honda Gold Wings, Harleys and Kawasaki Z1300s that went past. They all waved back, although some of them were clearly puzzled by my bike. I stayed with friends of friends in Boone that night, which had the distinction of being my first dry town in the USA. We had to drive eight miles to get across the county line and find a bar where we could spend the rest of the evening drinking jugs of Black & Tan.

The countryside in Georgia was dull and mostly flat. Atlanta promised to be a bit more interesting when I discovered that the Youth Hostel had

First sight of the Pacific in over 2½ years, and the end of the trip around the world. But there was still plenty to see after Lincoln City, Oregon

been demolished—and there certainly weren't any campsites around. I stayed in the YMCA, in a very definitely black neighbourhood, and when I went for an afterdinner walk, I was the only white person on the street and in the bar. No problem though, especially when it became known that I was Australian. I'm glad they hadn't heard of the White Australia Policy. ... Everyone in Georgia speaks with that seductive southern drawl. It makes an enquiry as to one's preferred beverage in a diner sound like an invitation to view the bedroom. ... Yes, I liked Georgia. My next breakfast, actually, was taken in a chain restaurant called a Huddle House and was awful. I promised myself I'd stick to the little private diners after that. They're almost always excellent value.

The fine for littering the roads in Georgia is $25, after a high in Connecticut and Florida of $500. It's still pretty clean, for all that, and the people are very friendly. A Mustang full of young ladies followed me for two or three miles while they figured out my number-plate and all the stickers on the back of the bike, then they went past tooting the horn, waving and throwing peace signs.

Another thunderstorm caught me down in Alabama and followed me almost to the campsite out on one of the sand islands, called Keys, off the coast. There were 'Don't feed the Alligators' signs up all over the site. Oh, boy. Can you imagine an alligator coming up and stealing your picnic basket? The men down here were all carefully haircut, and the women even more carefully made up. But I still found no hassles, in the bars or elsewhere—as long as I managed to keep the conversation off colour. Whites in the South are a long way from accepting blacks as

One of many flat tyres, this one on the Pacific coast of Oregon. It really pays to replace tubes occasionally ...

equals, and are very careful to make a point of that in conversation with strangers. As a visitor, I found myself in a difficult position, and I'm afraid I compromised by keeping my mouth shut. I pondered all this one morning over that great American institution, the bottomless cup of coffee, in Hazel's Diner in Gulf Shores. No conclusion emerged, I'm sorry to say, beyond the obvious fact that I ought to stay out of something I knew far too little about. That, much as I regret it, was my contribution to civil rights in the South.

Mobile was resplendent with magnolia and old Southern mansions, and the long ride along the coast to New Orleans rather reminded me of Australia. The road could have been running along Port Philip Bay, or through Brighton-le-Sands in Sydney, going by the architecture and the flora.

New Orleans was rather different, of course. I teamed up with Matt, a Canadian who pulled in at the YMCA at almost the same time. He was on a Honda CB900 Special, a bike rather better suited to US touring than poor old Hardly. Matt and I went out to do the town together. The Gumbo Shop came first—a restaurant specializing in the traditional

The author 'getting his kicks on Route 66'—actually just a can of Coors. Very little of the old Route 66 remains, superseded by freeways

Creole cooking—and was surprisingly cheap. Then we hit the hustle and bustle. First a walk up Bourbon Street, with its tourist glitter, and then a visit to Preservation Hall, one of the few places where genuine New Orleans Jazz is still played. There's no booze available, so our next stop was Pat O'Brien's Bar, next door, where we each put away a Hurricane, a monstrous $5 cocktail which seems to consist mostly of rum. At Sloppy Jim's, over a few glasses of draught Dixie Beer, we tried to collate our ideas of New Orleans. It's a strange town. The place is full of tourists, yet it doesn't feel like a tourist town. Everbody has a good time, except perhaps for the crowds in the assembly-line bars on Bourbon Street. Off the main drag, the people in the bars and restaurants are there to enjoy themselves—and they're not about to be cheated of it; as a couple we met in O'Brien's said: 'We're from Jackson, Mississippi, but when we want to have a good time, we come down here!'

I did my laundry the next day in a laundromat supervised by one of the descendants of Marie Laveau, the famous witch. At least I presume that she was a descendant—she looked and acted like it, and she was certainly in the right business. It was hot again when I braved the spaghetti of roads leading out of town and eventually over Lake Pontchartrain on the 24-mile-long causeway.

The way north was all friendly but obviously poor people, corpses of armadillos slaughtered by cars, and poorly surfaced but pretty little roads. Then I reached the Natchez Trace, another route like the Blue

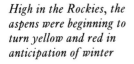

High in the Rockies, the aspens were beginning to turn yellow and red in anticipation of winter

Ridge Parkway, and followed that north to Nashville in serenity. I did stop off to pay my respects at Elvis Presley's birthplace in Tupelo. The suburb is now called Elvis Presley Heights. I visited Opryland in Nashville, a kind of Country & Western Disneyland, and had a good time. The one thing that annoyed me was that I had to pay as much as a car driver to park. This is fairly common in the US—there are no parking or toll concessions for bikes.

A few days later I reached Ann Arbor, Michigan, and another friend of a friend. Victoria and her parents welcomed me with open arms and supplied a sort of replacement home for a few days. I really needed it by this time, too. It does get lonely out on the road, even if you speak the local language. One sight in Ann Arbor that I will always remember is the sign at the Farmers' Market that says 'No pets, bicycles or solicitors'.

The bike got a much-needed and fast service, as well as a new chain. Then it took me north again, up through the Norman Rockwell country that makes up central Michigan, to Sleeping Bear Dunes on Lake Michigan. In the campsite that night I had a steady stream of visitors, fascinated by the sight of the little bike. I scored a dinner invitation, a gift of a kilo of smoked fish (fishing is big up here) and an evening sitting around drinking other people's beer. Very friendly. Not so friendly was the gunshop I saw the next day, offering free targets—large pictures of the Ayatollah Khomeini. I reached the Upper Peninsula of Michigan with a terrible hangover. I had been attempting to cure a cold with bourbon, successfully, but was paying for it. John from Boulder rode into the campsite that night on a BMW R60/5, which he'd come over to the east to buy. Bikes are much cheaper in the Eastern States than in California or in John's home state of Colorado. He had a story about being mugged, too. Apparently a 5ft tall mugger had approached John, who measured 6ft 4in, near Times Square and threatened him. 'He ran away pretty quickly', said John, 'when I pointed out the error of his ways. But you gotta give him credit. . . .'

It was a mining town once, but now Cripple Creek gets its gold from the pockets of tourists. My modern burro looks more contented than the old one in the poster!

174

I received the inevitable American invitation to come and stay before we parted in the morning, and took off a little before John. He passed me not long afterwards—the BMW had longer legs than the little Honda.

Upper Wisconsin was strange, with eerie abandoned-looking farms, rusting cars and run-down petrol stations along the highway. Things got better as I went farther west, and by the time I reached Janesville (the sign outside town just said 'Janesville—a friendly place') I felt as though I was in the prosperous Midwest you read about. Towns like New Ulm, Balaton and Florence remind you of the many nations that supplied the settlers here. Mind you, it's also pretty boring country. Flat as far as the eye can see. . . . That didn't change the next day, but it was pleasant just the same. First, in the diner in Lake Preston, there was a complete set of Australian banknotes in a frame over the bar. I asked the bloke next to me where they came from, and he thought about his answer for a while before saying: 'Feller that useta live here now lives there.' They're a quiet lot in the Midwest.

At my next petrol stop I was invited in for coffee and brownies and then, when I stopped to tighten the chain, the sidestand broke and the bike fell on my head. Fun all day! I slept in the campground in the Badlands that night, among the grotesque landforms that give the place its name. Spooky, with spires of soft rock reaching for the full moon, not a blade of grass or a bush on them.

The Harley shop in Rapid City was very helpful, and even managed to locate someone who would weld my sidestand back for a few dollars.

The Black Hills were pretty, especially after the long run over the Great Plains, but they're rather spoilt by dozens of tacky tourist traps. These fill the side of the road leading to Mount Rushmore and consist of such things as The Life of Jesus Wax Museum. The famous faces on the mountain itself look rather funny for some reason. Most of the Black Hills is totally unspoilt, and I found myself a little free Forestry Service campsite, where I was joined by two other riders. One had a CX500, the

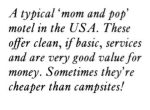

A typical 'mom and pop' motel in the USA. These offer clean, if basic, services and are very good value for money. Sometimes they're cheaper than campsites!

175

other an immaculate Harley Sportster. We lit a fire, drank what booze we had between us and watched the satellites passing over in the crystal night air. An elderly couple travelling in a camper joined us, and brought an enormous shopping bag full of fresh popcorn. What a night!

There's a system of balance in nature. After you've had a good time for a while, you get a bad time. Mine started the next morning with a flat tyre, and continued when the bike wouldn't start. Too high up, perhaps. We were a mile high. Much pushing finally got us under way, after I'd filled the tube with latex foam from an aerosol can. The bike laboured all that day against a strong headwind across Wyoming, the original cowboy country. Rolling grassy hills as far as I could see, broken by mostly dry water courses with names like Dead Horse Creek and Mad Woman Creek. It was overcast and chilly. But the sun came out the next day, and as I rode up to the Powder River Pass and Tensleep Canyon I thought of John Muir, the founder of the Sierra Club, who had said: 'There is something in the sight of the mountains that restores a man's spirit.'

I could have done with a little extra restoration in Basin, just on the other side of the mountains. The rear tyre was flat again, and I began the mammoth task of repairing the old tube. Mammoth because I kept pinching it while putting it back in. I wasn't yet used to the new set of tyre levers I'd bought, and the tube was very old. By the time the rear tyre held air again, the tube had six new patches on it and I retreated to the local bar to try to drown my sorrows. At least I found convivial company and a couple of good games of pool, and had my first taste of decent Coors beer—a significant improvement on the usual American slops. I also got a lot of sympathy for not being American, and specifically for not being from Wyoming. The entire clientele of the bar assured me that Wyoming was the best place in the whole world, even if Basin, with its population of 700, might be a bit slow. My road west from this little

The big parade at Aspendale. Known as a 'Motorcyclist's Convention', it attracts thousands of bikes—but sadly rather lacks the spirit of European or Australian rallies

oasis kept heading for a window in the thick general overcast, a window filled with sunshine and pretty little clouds. But I couldn't catch it, and it finally disappeared when I reached Cody, a town devoted to the memory of Buffalo Bill Cody, or at least devoted to the amount of tourist money that memory could bring in.

Up in the mountains once again, I found a bloke lying on the ground next to the most decrepit bike I have ever seen—and I've seen some decrepit bikes in my day, some of them mine. This was a 250cc Honda of indeterminate vintage, with one muffler tied to the rack and most parts held on either by grease or wire. The owner of this apparition bummed a few coke cans of petrol from me—this being the most convenient receptacle to drain the petrol into—and went cheerily on his way.

Shoshone Canyon provided some exciting riding the next day, and took me up to the gates of Yellowstone National Park, and the snow once more. It was disappointing to learn that all the bears had been moved up to the high country, but it appeared that they had been having trouble with the humans. There was no danger of my meeting any bears that night anyway; I checked into the Old Faithful Lodge. Snow had been forecast for the night, and my tent suddenly seemed awfully flimsy.

Yellowstone Park itself was beautiful, like a piece of the world just after the creation, but I wasn't particularly impressed by the Old Faithful geyser. One Japanese bloke was, though. He spent most of the evening sitting at the bar's picture window, a barely tasted glass of whisky in front of him, gazing at the geyser. My evening was rather profane—I celebrated New Year's Eve with the staff. A trifle odd seeing that it was 31 August. ... It appears that a few years ago a party of visitors were trapped by an early snowstorm towards the end of August. They reasoned that since they were stuck anyway, and it was white outside, they

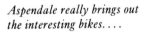

Aspendale really brings out the interesting bikes....

might as well celebrate Christmas. The staff have taken this up as a tradition, and there's always a Christmas and a New Year's Eve party towards the end of August.

I had a marvellous time meeting everybody, discussing politics, the MX system and the iniquity of the labour laws; all those things which are endlessly fascinating when you're drunk, getting more drunk and the surroundings feel good. One of the fascinating things I discovered that night was that if you're over 6ft 7in tall, you're safe from the draft. The army isn't set up to cope with people taller than that. So grow! All the celebrating must have disturbed my sense of direction, because I took the wrong road in the morning. Instead of heading for Craters of the Moon National Park, I found myself on the road to Missoula. I made the best of it anyway and enjoyed the sweeping wheat fields and later the enormous trees of Lolo Pass. Just over the pass, an elderly chap on a KZ400 with a sidecar waved me over to the side of the road and offered me a cup of coffee. We stood in the thin drizzle, drank coffee out of his thermos and compared travelling styles. He was travelling even more slowly than I!

Outside Lewiston I had another flat tyre. This time I replaced the tube, and the bike needed a new wheel bearing. The old one had been severly knocked around from having the wheel removed so often. The bike was running much better now that I was out of the high country. Perhaps it would have been worth while to change the jetting after all.

I didn't need any directions to get to Portland—just follow the Columbia River, right along the tops of the sheer cliffs that border its northern side. But once in Portland, I did need directions—just to find the post office. It seemed I had come to the wrong town. The first person I asked was a biker who had broken down on the freeway. He told me I wanted the exit two back. This on the freeway, where you can't turn around. After I'd found my way into town by myself, I asked a lady at

'Okay, I'm sitting on it. Now what do I do?' Someone's first encounter with a Harley-Davidson Sturgis, the belt-driven machine named after the big H-D rally

a street corner. She did her valiant best, but became totally incoherent within a few seconds. We both finally gave up. I then found the post office by myself, checked for mail, and made the mistake of asking for the road to the west. Firstly, he tried to talk me into going south. Then he told me to go down a certain street and turn left just *before* I could see the viaduct. *What* is the matter with Portland?

At Lincoln City, when I finally did reach the coast, I saw the Pacific for the first time since the beginning of the trip. In a way, my circum-navigation of the Earth was over. But of course the trip was far from over, so I headed off down the coast the next morning. I stopped quite early at a lookout to take a photo of the fog swirling in to bathe the foot of the cliffs. When I got back on the bike, it was once again those ominous few inches lower. Another flat rear tyre—and this time there was an enormous sliver of glass in my nice new tube. Out with the tyre levers once again . . .

The coast was lovely, with forests and cliffs and dunes and hills and enormous trees—and a family of moose in a meadow by the river. The Youth Hostel in Bandon, a well-preserved old fishing town, provided shelter for three days while I relaxed, reading and checking over the bike. A new chain was overdue, so I made a shopping trip into the local metropolis, Coos Bay. The Honda shop had a chain, and a small super-market had some beer in white cans just marked 'Beer'. It was explained to me that this was what was known as a 'generic' product—no brand name, no advertising, and therefore a low price. I bought a six pack. On the way back to Bandon I also picked an enormous plastic shopping bag full of blackberries. I was just congratulating myself on how well every-thing was going when the rear chain broke. Well, well. When will I learn not to congratulate myself? It was rather convenient that I was carrying the brand-new replacement in my tank box.

My new-found friend Larry thought that story was very funny when I told him in the bar that night. Larry was an extremely laid-back ex-Marine, whose wife owned one of the three bars in town. He explained to me why he was happy with his life. 'You know the story about the perfect wife being a deaf and dumb nymphomaniac who owns a bar? Well, look, my wife may not be deaf and dumb, but she owns this place, and as far as the rest is concerned. . . .'

On down the coast, and past the gloomy but impressive hulk of Humburg Mountain, a block of stone between the road and the sea. I was in the redwood forests by now, which presented a problem in photography. Even with the widest lens I carried, I had to put the camera up quite a distance from the tree if I wanted to get both the top and bottom in, as well as myself standing at the base. So I'd put the camera on the tripod, set the self-timer and run like hell to get to the tree before the shutter went off. I succeeded most of the time. Maybe it was the majesty of the trees, but I started to do some rather serious thinking about what this trip had taught me, and how I had changed in the last two and a half years. I could come up with very little, except that I missed Annie badly. It's probably not so much that there's little to learn on this kind of trip ... it's more that I'm incorrigible. After all, I'd coped pretty well with all the different cultures ... hadn't I? I had looked forward to discussing all this with Ted Simon, who had written a marvellous book called *Jupiter's Travels* about his own circumnavigation of the globe. Ted now lived in San Francisco, and mutual acquaintances had given me his address and telephone number. But when I rang, it was to discover that he had just become a father—and swapping ideas about bike travel was the farthest thing from his mind. I could hardly blame him!

When I got out of the phone box, the bike refused to start. The poor little 250XL had been mistreated for so long that it was finally rebelling. Even pushing wouldn't do it. As it happened, the phone box was outside the Municipal Offices for the small town I was in, so I went in there looking for pushers. The Sheriff, Deputy Sheriff and the Fire Chief all lent a hand, and the bike—out of respect, I guess—fired straight away.

Through the coastal fog, I rode the last few miles into San Francisco. The fog was eerie, somehow—I had the constant feeling that there was an enormous eye, just above the fog, looking for me. California was beginning to affect me, I guess. They do say that the place has more religious nuts than any other place on Earth. Maybe it's catching. Once

Erik Hunstein and his wife, from Germany, had ridden their Moto Guzzi outfit all the way to Alaska, and were on their way to Mexico when I met them

in the city, having crossed a Golden Gate Bridge whose upper beams were invisible in the same fog, I started looking for a bike shop to service the XL.

The Honda dealer's Service Manager was dubious. She indicated her crew of mechanics and said: 'These prima donnas only like to put new bits on new bikes,' something that the XL definitely wasn't. But she sent me down to Cycle Source, a small service shop run by the inimitable Jack Delmas. Jack is an ex-cop, and one of the friendliest, most helpful blokes I've ever met. His staff aren't far behind, either—Chris, on the spares counter, and Eddie, in the workshop, both helped me out. The shop was like a little home away from home. Eddie also got the bike running—and starting—beautifully—all at very reasonable rates. I celebrated by doing wheelies up the steep streets of San Francisco, racing the cable cars.

SF is one of those very rare cities that feels good. Fishermen's Wharf is just a tourist trap, but North Beach is full of great bars, with good music and imported beer. Although why they bother importing Bass is beyond me. . . . Then it was time to turn east again, over the Bay Bridge and through Oakland and all the little valley towns to Yosemite National Park.

If Yellowstone is beautiful, Yosemite is exquisite. The soaring cliffs, yellow meadows and dark pine forests set each other off so well that the place hardly looks real. All development has been done carefully, and presents a low profile. The park is like a natural garden, from the delicacy of Bridal Veil Falls to the brute mass of Half Dome. Despite the lateness of the season, the campgrounds in the valley were full, so I camped in one of the free sites up in the hills. Smoky Jack campground was very pleasant in the half-dark, with campfires and stars both twinkling away. Despite the cold night, I slept well—no doubt partly due to the good offices of Jim Beam. Mono Lake was a little disappointing; its strange rock formations didn't really live up to the publicity. But I was thoroughly enchanted with an extremely attractive 'flagperson' with one of the road repair gangs I met on the way south. Women are now a common sight in road gangs in America, but they seem mostly to do the less strenuous work. That's changing too, though. I saw a number of female tractor drivers.

At Lone Pine I turned onto the roller-coaster that passes for a road down to Death Valley. From 5000ft it goes nearly to sea level, then back to 5000, down to two, back to nearly five, and then down to Furnace Creek, 178ft below sea level. True to form, it was hot—over 37°C—and it didn't cool down much at night. There were some German travellers camped next to me, and although I got some sleep on top of a picnic table in my underpants, they tossed and turned all night. Australian conditioning finally comes in handy!

I had a strong headwind the next day, and was nearly blown off Zabriskie Point lookout. But when I turned left at the ghost town of Death Valley Junction the wind was at my back and helped me along. The whole area is very impressive for its total desolation—over square mile after square mile not a blade of grass grows. It must have been a tough life working in the mines here.

Las Vegas spreads its rather unattractive tentacles far out into the desert. Housing developments go up on the flat, windy plain and some attempt is made to civilize it all by pouring great quantities of water into the ground to grow a bit of anaemic lawn. I much prefer the desert itself. The town is great fun, with its amazing architecture, combination loan offices/motels/wedding chapels/divorce offices, acres of neon and single-minded people. Something seemed odd to me about all the casinos, and it took a while before I'd worked out what it was. Unlike the equivalents in Europe, Las Vegas casinos were not styled like palaces or upper-class residences. Here, they were styled in Ultimate Surburban—their exteriors like a hamburger joint gone mad, their interiors like a suburban tract house owned by a surburban millionaire. Lots of flash, but no taste. Tremendous fun, all of it.

In the bizarre, broken-down little town of Chloride, I asked the toothless old petrol-pump attendant where the campsite was. He pointed to the top of a distinctly bare hill off in the distance, and I decided to push on to Kingman instead. I followed one of the few remaining stretches of Route 66 in the morning, and rode through Coconino County, the home of Krazy Kat in the famous thirties comic strip of the same name. Meanwhile, dozens of grasshoppers hit my legs as I rode along—it was almost like riding through gravel as they rattled against my shins. There seemed to be quite a plague of them.

Still in beautiful sunshine, I rode up to the Grand Canyon. The bike was still running well and lapping up the excellent roads of Arizona and Nevada. But it was getting a little hard to start again, so whenever I pulled up to take a look at the Canyon, I tried to find a slope to make clutch starting easier. Despite these concerns, I still found the Canyon marvellous. The sheer size is overpowering, and it takes quite a while before the mind can take in its scale. It's very pretty, too, but it reminded me irresistibly of an enormous layer cake that's been attacked by monster mice. From here, I turned north-east towards Durango and the Rockies. The old Indians at the roadside stalls where I stopped to buy turquoise souvenirs had the most awe-inspiring faces I think I've ever seen. Lined and sombre, their faces reminded me of photos of Sitting Bull.

The road past the bald head of Engineer Mountain and up to the 11,000ft pass leading to Silverton was great. Quite aside from the fact that I was enjoying having corners again—despite its weight and nearly worn-out shock absorbers, the XL was fun on winding roads—I also got an altitude high. This happens to me occasionally when I get too high up, and I start making faces, singing, cracking jokes and laughing like crazy—all to myself. It also helped that I was back in the lovely Rockies, with forests of aspens and conifers on the steep slopes and that marvellous cold, clean air. Some of the aspens were already beginning to turn from green to gold. Winter was on its way. I hurried to get to Denver, where I expected mail to be waiting for me, but of course the best-laid plans of mice and bears. . . .

Just outside Conifer, some 40 miles from Denver, my throttle cable broke. I was on the very edge of the huge rampart of mountains that leads down to Denver, so I tried coasting. I got 18 miles before I ran out of hill! Then—at Bear Lake, to add to injury—I finally had to give in and switch the return cable with the broken one. This gave me a throttle control, but of course it now turned the opposite way—to accelerate, I had to turn the throttle away from me. Lots of fun in peak-hour Denver traffic!

By now it was too late to go to the post office, and when I got there in the morning there was no mail for me anyway. It's always a bit depressing when you're on the road for a while and don't get mail. You really feel lonely. But I still had the address of John-with-the-BMW, whom I'd met in Michigan, so I went up to Boulder to stay with him. In traditional American style, I was made most welcome by all the inhabitants of his house and spent a cheerful few days there. Boulder is full of musicians and has an excellent library. I loafed and read and listened to music.

My mail was waiting for me when I got to Denver again a week later, and my bliss was nearly complete. But I was still missing Annie, very much.

Down to Colorado Springs along the row of frozen combers that make up the eastern edge of the Rocky Mountains, and then up and around Pike's Peak to Cripple Creek. An early mining settlement, this little town

Now that's the American Way of touring! An all-Harley outfit ready to take on the world

has now suffered the fate of all picturesque places in the US—it's become a tourist trap and derives its substance from the buses. It was still pretty, though, and the scenery on the way even more so. Some of the trees were actually changing from gold to bright scarlet and the slopes were marbled with the different shades.

Sand Dunes National Memorial, an enormous dune formed by wind forced to drop its load of dust and sand by a mountain range, was not as impressive as the booklet had suggested, so I took my leave again and headed for New Mexico. Leaving Kit Carson's old fort to one side (he was the local hero here), I made Taos in the early afternoon. This has to be just about the ultimate in tourist towns—it gives the impression of having been built exclusively for the trade. Not that it isn't pretty, it just seems so phoney. Perhaps I shouldn't talk. I only spent an hour there. I slept up in the hills above Santa Fe that night, deep in another world. Everyone here speaks Spanish, the shop signs are in Spanish and the fluorescent Coors advertisements all say 'cerveza' instead of 'beer'. I felt as though I'd made it to Mexico. In another sad case of prejudice, a white Anglo-Saxon-etc. American I asked wouldn't tell me where any of the local bars were. He didn't think I really ought to drink with 'those people'.

From Santa Fe I took the back roads to Albuquerque and found myself back up in the mountains. It was drizzly and cold, too, but the road was well surfaced, narrow and twisty; I had a good time here. I also stopped in a weird little town called Madrid. It had obviously not long since been a ghost town, but now a great crew of hippies was busy restoring, shoring up and beautifying the wonky-looking timber houses.

On the way to Ruidoso and the Aspencade Motorcyclists Convention, I began to worry about the chain again. I'd had to tighten it rather frequently—neither of the chains I'd bought in the US lasted very well—and now the bike was jerking quite noticeably. I had all sorts of fantasies

Eighteen wheels meet two in the desert of Nevada. The XL did a very commendable job in hauling me, and all my gear, through high temperatures and great elevations

about bent countershafts (silly) and twisted sprockets (sillier). Riding was becoming unpleasant. I made it to Ruidoso anyway, and spent a relaxed couple of days watching the bikes roll in. I'd been in touch with Honda, and they had expressed an interest in having my XL250 on their stand at the trade show, so, once the show started, I spent my evenings down there talking to the visitors—who found it very difficult to believe that anyone could be crazy enough to ride a 250 around the world.

Days were spent drinking with my newly acquired friends Norman—who left his little dog Honda guarding their Gold Wing—and Bob, who'd ridden to the show on one of the very few two-strokes around. Nothing much was going on, rather a dissappointment after the bustle of European rallies, but it was great to talk to so many people, from so many walks of life, who were all devoted to motorcycling. I was a little surprised to see relatively few Harleys compared with the waves of Gold Wings that inundated the place.

I rode the new Harley Sturgis, and was very impressed with the belt drives, and spent a lot of time admiring the custom bikes. Unfortunately, they mostly looked as though they'd been put together out of three different mail-order catalogues. There was not really much variety. The trikes were spectacular, but once again there was little variety among them. On the third day, I won the 'Longest Distance—Solo Male Rider' trophy, which still hangs proudly on the wall of my office. Then it was off again—a straight run for the coast. Every trip has a limited lifespan and after 11 weeks this one was gasping its last. So it was out onto the Interstate, a road I generally avoided, and off.

Seventeen miles from Yuma the steering went heavy. Inspection showed that the patch we had put on the front tube in the Khyber Pass had lifted. It was well over 35°C, there was no shade, and in fact it was very similar to the conditions in which the tube had first given out. It went flat again just outside Yuma, so I had a new tube fitted. I rather begrudged that now, seeing we were so close to the end of the trip, but I couldn't be bothered with any more flats. In El Centro I also found an excellent bike shop, where they located a good second-hand Tsubaki chain to replace my old, worn-out one. So I was ready to face the last stretch with confidence!

The road to the coast was most enjoyable, through rugged hills on an excellent surface. In San Diego a solid wall of smog was waiting for me. I made my way down to the Pacific—nice to see an old friend again—and watched the huge oily rollers coming in all the way from Australia.

Up the coast into the rat's nest of freeways that is Los Angeles, and a stop at the *Road Rider* magazine office, where I was received very well and offered the use of a typewriter. I spent the last few days before my flight was due wandering around, by bike mostly, and sightseeing. I found Hollywood especially interesting—not so much the homes of the stars as Hollywood Boulevard. Then I had lunch with the friendly folk from Honda USA, entrusted my little bike to them for storage and climbed aboard the plane with the big red kangaroo on the tail.

I spent the flight planning the next trip....

Epilogue

Ah, yes, the next trip. The funny thing about touring is that we have yet to meet a rider returning from one triumphant tryst with the open road who isn't already planning the next assignation. It takes but a little while for this courtship of the concrete to accelerate into a full-blown affair with the asphalt, and for many it's love at first sight. Sure, there must be a few would-be motorcycle tourists who try it once and decide it's not for them. That's understandable. And certainly there are times when even the most ardent touring fan bows to family considerations and takes the car, or crashes out with the kids for a week in the Canaries. That can be fun too. But despite these diversions most of us are hooked for life.

Exactly why we're hooked is hard to say. A lot of writers have tried to pin down the reasons and come up gasping for words. Others have come close. Robert Louis Stevenson might have had motorcycling in mind when he wrote: 'To travel hopefully is a better thing than to arrive.' A little ahead of his time, perhaps, but as true today as it was then. Roger Hull, the bard of the American touring motorcyclist, puts it this way: 'It's the going. I mosey across the miles, mingle with the elements, merge with the macrocosm. See and feel for myself what others may have seen and experienced before me. A wandering cowboy, I ... with an emotional genealogy which is suspected of linkage back to Cortez or Columbus or Marco Polo or to any other free spirit whose vision tended to focus on that which lay beyond what his eyes could see.

'Touring is a lonely feat; we are solitary seekers, wanderers sensitive to our physical surroundings, while we live mostly inside our heads.'

Therein lies the greater part of the magic: while touring on a motorcycle your body and your senses are open to an ever-changing battery of stimuli, and your mind in its solitude is the freer to savour them. The combined effect is spellbinding, and that's what keeps the touring rider coming back for more again and again.

While the horizons of the world have been unfolding across these pages we have started touring in our back yard, wandered farther afield, crossed whole continents and finally completed a circumnavigation of the globe by motorcycle. If you have recognized your own experiences in any of these places then we are flattered and hope you have been prompted to ride more distant roads, if all we have done is awaken a free spirit to the delights of motorcycle touring then we are truly proud.

186

Appendix

Motorcycle package tour organizers

NORTH AMERICA

Canadian Alpine Tours Ltd
202–325 Howe Street
Vancouver
British Columbia
Canada V6C 1Z7
(tel: 604–669 0313)

Western Adventures Inc
6141 Camino Almonte
Tucson
Arizona 85718
USA
(tel: 602–299 4691)

Motorcycle Tours of America
407 Rio Grande NW
Albuquerque
New Mexico 87104
USA

EUROPE

Alpine Motorcycle Tours
PO Box 3041
Mission Viejo
California 92690
USA
(tel: 714–837 1392)

Mike Von Thielmann's BMW
  Rally
11379 Matinal Circle
San Diego
California 92127
USA
(tel: 714–487 9890)

World Motorcycle Tours
778 Bloomfield Avenue
Caldwell
New Jersey 07006
USA
(tel: 201–226 9065)

International Motorcycle Touring
  Club Rally/Tours
5118 Rolling Hills Court
Tampa
Florida 336
USA
(tel: 813–988 6561)

Bob Beach's Motorcycle Adventures
2763 West River Parkway
Grand Island
New York 14072
USA
(tel: 716-773 4960)

Other useful addresses
International Motorcyclists Tour Club
105 Mackenzie Crescent
Burncross
Sheffield S30 4UR
England

International Tourer's Club
112 Queens Road
Nuneaton
Warwickshire CV11 5LS
England

Index

AA 35
Acireale 129
Adelaide 53
Agadir 114
Agra 73
Ain Salah 122
Albany 53
Alexandropoulis 93, 139
Alfama 107
Algeciras 108
Alicante 105
Amalfi 38, 40, 45
Amersfoort 96
Amritsar 77
Anamur 91, 142
Anatolian Plateau 144
Ankara 144–5
Antalya 152
Ann Arbor 174
Antrim, Co 17
Aosta 30, 38, 39
Apollo Bay 52
Ardrossan 24
Arklow 13
Arles 107
Armidale 49
Aspencade Motorcycle
    Convention 152, 157,
    167, 184
Assisi 131
Athens 119, 137, 139
Atlanta 152
Aughavanagh 11, 17
Ayutthaya 65

BMW 13, 16, 33, 85, 91, 93,
    94, 107, 148, 149, 151–
    4, 161, 175
    1000 32
    R45 136
    R60 49, 133
    R60/5 174
    R100S 18, 20, 114, 115,
    139, 142–5, 151

BSA 59
    M20
    Gold Star 163
Baghdad 74
Baja 107
Balaton 175
Balla 25
Ballina 49
Bamian 80, 83, 85
Band 179
Bangkok 64–7
Bannockburn 24
Barcelona 104
Barinsdale 164
Basin 176
Bayonne 103
Bay of Biscay 146
Bear Lake 183
Beziers (tyres) 102
Biarritz 102–3
Birganj 71
Bitola 135
Black Hills 175
Black Sea 81
Bloody Foreland 17
Blue Ridge Parkway 170
Bluff Knoll 55
Bodnath 70
Bois 96, 99
Bologna 30
Bonn 41
Boston 164
Boulder 174, 183
Boulogne 97
Bourton-on-the-Water 23
Bridge of Allan 24
Briggs, Annie 152
Brighton-le-Sands 171
British Motorcyclists
    Federation (BMF) 16,
    28, 156
Brisbane 164
Brittas Bay 17
Brucoli 128

Brunswick 96, 149
Bucharest 147
Budapest 148
Ben Bulban 18

Cadiz 108
Calafia 155
Calais 29, 35
Calcutta 77
Callander 25
Caltanisetta 128
Camargue 101
Canakkale 140
Canberra 135
Cape Cod 164
Cappadocia 89
Carcassonne 102
Carry le Rouet 101
Carson, Kit 184
Casablanca 113
Caspian Sea 87
Cassino
Castel Gandolfo 43
Castel Fusana 43
Catania 127–9
Ceduna 53, 55
Ceuta 109, 111
Chamonix 39, 40
Chandigar 74
Chartwell 22
Chechaouen 111
Chesapeake 169
Chieng Mai 65
Chipping Norton 23
Conifer 183

Dalkey 17
Danube 148
Dead Horse Creek 176
Death Valley 181
Delhi 73–4
Delmas, Jack 181
Delphi 135

Denver 168, 182, 183
Desert of Death (Dasht-i-
    Dargo) 82
Devon 22
Dijon 29, 30, 39
Djeema el Fna 116
Dogubayazit 88
Donegal, Co 16–18
Dublin 11, 16–18, 21, 97
Dublin Motorcycle Tour
    Club 13
Dubrovnik 94, 133, 134
Ducati 151
    450 38
    900 151
    GT750 33
Dun Laoghaire 17, 21

EEC 35
Edinburgh 24
Egli-Kawasaki 40, 151
El Centro 152, 185
El Golea 120–1, 123
El Kelaa 117
El Oued 123
Enfield 350 77
Enna 128
Epernay 36
Ephesus 141
Epidaurus 136
Erzurum 88, 89
Escondido 154

Farrah River 86
Fes 118
Fisherman's Wharf 181
Fishguard 21, 97
Flinders Range 53
Florence 31, 42, 43, 175
Folkstone 149
Fort Augustus 25
Fort William 25

Gallipoli 40
Galway 18
Geelong 52
Genova 29, 30, 38
Ghardia 121
Ghazipur 69, 72
Ghazni 86
Ghorakpur 71
Giants Causeway 17
Gibellina 128
Glasgow 24
Gippsland 52
Glen Coe 25
Glen of the Downs 17
Glencoe 25
Glenmalure 17
Gol e Sahra 87, 169
Golden Gate Bridge 181
Göreme 89, 144, 146
Granada 105, 108
Grand Canyon 182
Gravesend 23
Great Australian Bight 54
Great Ridgeway 22
Great St. Bernard Pass 40,
    41
Great Western Erg 123
Greenwich Village 160
Guinness 17, 49, 61, 97
Gulf Shores 171

Had Yai 63
Hamburg 96
Harley-Davidson 136, 153-
    6, 170
    Electra Glide 40, 41, 93,
        151, 152
    FLH Classic 155
    Tour Glide 152
    Sportster 152
    Sturgis 185
    WLA 49, 61
Harris (Isle of) 25
Hazona 123
Herat 86-7
Holyhead 21, 23
Honda 90 11
    125 13
    400/4 22, 102, 112
    450 56
    500 43, 91
    500/4 61
    750 13
    900 42
    CBX 16, 23, 32
    CX500 33, 154
    CB900 172

XL125 125
XL250 34, 50, 52, 75, 82,
    91, 95, 97, 115, 164,
    166-7, 180-1
Benly CB92 Sports 11
Gold Wing 13, 32, 59,
    151, 152, 154-7, 170,
    185
Honda USA 185
Hora 136
Humberg-Untu 179

Ifrane 118
Islamabad 81
Isle of Man 23-4
Istanbul, 91, 145
Izmir 141

Jallalabad 82
Jamaica 161
Jammu 75, 76
Janesville 175
Jawa-Yezdi 75
Jhansi 73
Johore Baharu 59
Joyce, James 17, 18
Jupiter's Travels 180

Kabul 85
Kabul Gorge 82
Kabul River 82
Kalabaka 135
Kalamata 136
Kale 142
Kalkhan 91
Kampar 61
Kandahar 86
Kashmir 75, 78
Katmandu 67, 69, 70
Kavala 93
Kawasaki 1000 53, 164
    Z400 178
    Z750 164
    Z1300 32, 41, 153-6, 170
Kayseri 77
Kelat 86
Kemer 91
Kerry Co 14, 17
Keys 171
Khajuraho 66, 73
Khyber 81
Khyber Pass 78, 185
Killarney 17
Killiney Hill 17
Kingston 163
Kirsehir 144
Kotor Bay 94
Kotor Hill 94

Krauser 20
Kreider Florett 50cc 93
Ksar es Souk 117
Kauntuan 60-2
Kusadasi 141
Kyle of Lochalsh 25
Kyleakin 25

La Ciocat 100
Lahore 66
Lake Albert 53
Lake Michigan 174
Lake Phewa 71
Lake Preston 175
Lake Tuz 89
Lakes Entrance 52
Lamezia Terme 130
Lamia 135-6
Land-Rover 16, 87, 123
Laragh 17, 41
Laverda 151
Le Havre 21, 99
Les Rousses 29
Les Stes Maries 107
Lewiston 178
Li 65
Lincoln City 170, 179
Lisbon 107
Liverpool 21, 23
Loch Leven 25
Lolo Pass 178
London 21, 30, 57, 96, 99,
    119
Lone Pine 181
Lorne 52
Lower Slaughter 23
Los Angeles 152
Lugano 95
Luneberg 96

Mad Woman Creek 176
Mallaig 25
Maku 87, 88
Manhattan 159, 163
Martignes 101
Martigny 41
Marseilles 100-1
Mashad 87
Martil 111
Mayer, Bruce 154
Mazar 83
Meknes 111-13
Melbourne 49, 52
Mersin 90, 144
Mersing 60
Messina 129
Meteora 135

Metzlers 102
Michigan 183
Middle Eastern Travel
    Magazine 123
Milan 30
Milazzo 129
Milo, Prince of Montenegro
    18-20
Mirzapur 72
Missoula 178
Mobile 171
Mohammedia 113
Mol, Michael 14, 116, 119,
    137-44, 145, 146
    Cathy 14, 116, 119, 137-
    46
Mont Blanc 30, 39, 40
Moreton-in-the-Marsh 23
Morgan 41
Morello 97
Morini 350 151
Morrocco 100, 109
Motherwell 24
Moto Guzzi 93, 104, 151
    850 30
    V7 Ambassador 13
    Le Mans 40, 151
Motorcycle Rider 153
Motorcycle Sport 153
Motorcycle Weekly 152
Mount Ararat 88
Mount Etna 129
Mount Gambier 53
Mount Rushmore 175
Mughal 76
Murray River 53

Nabeul 124
Nagarkot 70
Naples 38, 42, 45
Nashville 174
Nenasi 60
Nepal 61, 67
Nevshehir 89
New Forest 22
New Orleans 172
New South Wales 49
New York 159, 160, 164,
    166
Newman's Rocks 54
Newport Jazz Festival 166
Newry 16
Nigde 89
Nogales 152, 153
Norseman 55
Northern Ireland 16, 17
Norton 59, 93

Notre Dame du Rugby 103
Nullarbor 53, 114
Nuremburg 149

Ohio Canal 169
Ohrid 135
Old Forge 163
Olympia 136
Orleans 166
Ostend 149
Ostia 43
Otocac 133
Oujda 119
Ourzazate 116, 117
Oxfordshire 22

Pamplona 103
Pamukkale 141, 142
Paris, 35, 96
Passau 149
Patong Beach 63
Pec 94
Perth 54, 55
Pemberton 55
Penang 61, 66, 89
Pekan 60
Phangnga 63
Phitsanlok 66
Phuket Island 63
Pike's Peak 183
Piraeus 136
Plitvice 133
Pompeii 42, 45, 130
Ponte Vecchio 42
Pookara 53
Port Philip Bay 171
Portland 178
Portroe 97
Powder Creek Pass 176
Preston, Bruce 16, 19
   Brenda 19
Prizren 94
Pulchwoki 70

Queensland 27, 49, 56

RAC 35
Rabat 113
Ramsgate 29, 35
Raub 61
Rawalpindi 66
Reims 36
Renault 4CV 140
Rhine Valley 45
Ring of Kerry 97
Rishikesh 74

Road Rider 157, 167, 185
Rocco di Papa 43
Rome 21, 28, 31, 42, 43, 45,
   47, 130
Ross, John 24
Rosslare 97, 21
Roundstone 18
Roundwood 17
Royal National Park 51
Ruidoso 152, 167, 184

Sadao 63, 67
Sahara 117, 121
Salerno 130
Sally Gap 17
Salzburg 139
San Diego 185
San Giovanni 130
San Marino 131
San Sebastian 103
Sand Dunes National
   Memorial 184
Sanglas 500 105
Sante Fe 184
Saraburi 67
Satna 72
Sciacca 128
Scylla 130
Selinunte 128
Senj 133
Sens 100
Setubal 107-8
Seville 105, 108
Shenandoah Hills 170
Shoshone Canyon 177
Siddhartha 71
Sidi Moussa 114
Sierra Nevada 105
Silifke 90
Silverton 182
Simbales 108
Simla 74
Simon, Ted 180
Singapore 55-60
Skopje 133, 134, 135, 136
Sleeping Bear Dunes 174
Slunj 133
Smoky Bay 53
Snowdonia 23
Sochiro Honda 57, 95
Songeur 121
Sonkghla 63
St Bernard Pass 95
St Gotthard Pass 95
St Sever 103
Stillargan 13

Stirling 24
Stirling Ranges 55
Stonehenge 22
Stow-on-the-Wold 23
Strabane 17
Streaky Bay 53
Sukothai 66
Suzuki 50 59
   70 59
   125 115
   GS550 40
   GS750 99, 100, 102, 115,
      130
   GS850 153
   GS1000 153
Swansea 21
Swayambu 70
Sydney 17, 49, 51, 55, 159
Sydney University
   Motorcycle Club 51
Syracuse 128

Taddert 1]7
Tailem Bend 53
Tak 65
Tamanrasset 119
Taza 119
Tehran 87
Tensleep 176
Thap Sakae 64
Thaso 39
Thebes 136
Thessalonika 94
Thoen 65
Thoreau, Henry David 164
Tiaret 121
Tichka Pass 116
Tidal River 52
Tinggi 59
Titograd 94, 133-4, 136
Tlemcen 121
Tor Khan 118
Toulouse 102
Trabzon 89
Trapani 127
Trieste 95
Triumph Bonneville 152
Troy 141
Tucson 153
Tunis 122
Tupelo 174
Twelve Bens 18
Tyndrum 25

Uchisar 144
Udampur 75

Uffington Castle 22
Ulster 17
Umbria 131
Upper Peninsula 174
Upper Slaughter 23

Vale of Evesham 23
Valencia 105
Vallee d'Aosta 38
Varanasi 72
Veliko Tarnovo 146
Venice 131
Vermont 164
Verona 95
Vetter 100, 155
Vias 102
Vicenza 95
Vienna 149
Vietri 45
Villa d'Este 129
Villiers 67
Vinaroz 103

Washington 169
Westerham 22
Wexford 13
White Horse 22
Whitman, Walt 167
William Bay 55
Wilson's Promontory 52
Windermere 24
Wollongong 51
Woodhenge 22
Woodstock 23

Yamaha 70 61
   650 91
   500 twin 112, 116
   750 Custom 11
   DT125 77
   XS500 125
   XS 750 33, 40, 43, 112,
      153
   XS1100 32, 99, 100-2,
      105, 107, 108, 114, 115,
      127-38, 131, 139, 140-
      1, 153-4
   XT 500 50, 88, 119
Yamuna River 74
Yellowstone National Park
   177, 181
Yeppoon 49
Yosemite Valley 169, 181
Yuma 185

Zagreb 133
Zurich 95